W9-ADH-253

Reading Wide Awake

Politics, Pedagogies, and Possibilities

EDUCATION LIBRARY
UNIVERSITY OF KENTUCKY

Reading Wide Awake

Politics, Pedagogies, and Possibilities

Patrick Shannon

Foreword by Jeffrey D. Wilhelm

Teachers College, Columbia University
New York and London

Edc

LB
1050.2
.S434
2011

Published by Teachers College Press, 1234 Amsterdam Avenue, New York, NY
10027

Copyright © 2011 by Teachers College, Columbia University

All rights reserved. No part of this publication may be reproduced or transmitted
in any form or by any means, electronic or mechanical, including photocopy,
or any information storage and retrieval system, without permission from the
publisher.

Library of Congress Cataloging-in-Publication Data

Shannon, Patrick, 1951–
    Reading wide awake : politics, pedagogies, and possibilities / Patrick
    Shannon ; foreword by Jeffery D. Wilhelm.
        p. cm.
    Includes bibliographical references and index.
    ISBN 978-0-8077-5242-5 (pbk. : alk. paper)
        1. Reading—Social aspects—United States. 2. Literacy—Political aspects—
    United States. 3. Books and reading—United States. 4. Democracy and
    education—United States. I. Title.
    LB1050.2.S434   2011
    306.4'880973—dc23   2011016835

ISBN 978-0-8077-5242-5 (paper)

Printed on acid-free paper
Manufactured in the United States of America

18   17   16   15   14   13   12   11   8   7   6   5   4   3   2   1

Contents

Foreword

Shannon makes a case here for a particular kind of reading—a kind of context-sensitive reading necessary for wide-awake civic engagement, for meaningful social action, and for democracy itself. He argues that this kind of reading goes well beyond that of the "social competence" promoted by society and schools, and calls for a kind of reading—of all "texts" and of the world itself—that makes use of "sociological imagination." He contextualizes his argument in the explicit political discourse of our current day, as well as in the more implicit controlling discourses of our consumeristic culture.

This wide-awake, sociologically imaginative reading requires readers to understand how they are being positioned, to consider the "intelligence" and interests behind textual production, to make choices and take responsible actions.

As I read the newspaper this very morning I was struck by what I personally regard as a "main danger." I am reading about the efforts on the part of billionaires—and their newly formed entities (protected now as individuals under the Supreme Court's recent "Citizens United" finding) like Karl Rove's "Crossroads America" and the groups funded by billionaires Charles and David Koch—who are currently working to eliminate the collective bargaining rights of American teachers and other public servants. I am watching the television ads and the news about unfolding teacher protests, and I wonder how these "texts" are socially and historically constructed, positioning me and my values, telling me what to think without revealing their real reasoning or who will benefit. I worry about their message, but even more about their largely hidden power. What are the unfiltered readings of this situation by the less powerful? I find myself wondering if we as a people have enough knowledge of labor history and enough imagination about how power operates to comprehend what has happened in the past, and what may in the future happen if we lose particular hard-won civil rights and privileges for common people in favor of the "real special interests" of supranational corporations. I wonder what I should decide about these issues; how I should participate. As Shannon argues: "We cannot be apathetic and democratic simultaneously."

But I cavil. Suffice it to say that even if I am wrong about this "main danger," limited as I am by personal experience and perspective, I am still impressed that Patrick Shannon has helped me to "read" and think about the world with "hyper and pessimistic activism." I am also compelled to mention that, at this particular moment in cultural history, the book you hold in your hands is essential stuff. It's especially important at this moment in *educational* history, with the implementation of the Common Core State Standards. So much of what Shannon promotes works to meet the CCSS in both letter and spirit—e.g., understanding how and why different kinds of texts are made, and how they are constructed to create certain effects in readers.

As with all educational initiatives, the success of the CCSS will be determined not by its vision but by its implementation, influenced by how its textuality is conveyed. I dearly hope the CCSS will be put into practice, as is implied throughout the document, in ways that foreground all reading and composing as acts of agency in ways consistent with what Shannon proposes here. I'd go so far as to suggest that *Reading Wide Awake* should be required reading for all educators working to implement the CCSS, the greatest opportunity for promoting a real thinking curriculum that I have seen in my 30 years as an educator.

I was not only tremendously impressed with this book; I was inspired by it. I believe that democracy in this country is under threat from many forces: unbridled lobbying from moneyed interests, advertising, a stream of unedited dross from the Internet and other media . . . but even more importantly from our lack of awareness and capacity to comprehend causes and correlations, open-mindedness to different perspectives, and the ability to infer implicit patterns of influence and effect and to critique in ways that also offer positive visionary alternative possibilities. I worry that we do not culturally cultivate nor educate for the "sociological imagination," but I celebrate that we *could* do so.

I am amazed, as Shannon so eloquently puts it, that "personal choices and the negotiations of social choices are what make democracy possible and keep it vital. For educators, this could mean that our hopes for the potential roles for reading in our lives are tied to inquiries into our reading practices and the recognition that those practices domesticate as well as liberate us (and those we teach)." To make such choices, and to make the choices and resulting actions meaningful, requires conscious competence and wide-awakeness to how texts manipulate us to our benefit or cost.

I believe that teaching is arguably the most important career one can undertake. I believe this with particular passion right now because of the challenges currently facing the human race and all of creation. I agree with Shannon that there is reason to be positive. After all, what have we actually tried to honestly address the challenges before us? And I agree with Shannon that we should pin our hopes on reading. I positively shivered with delight as I read what he so persuasively presented in this regard: It summed up beautifully the reasons for my own dedication to a career as a literacy educator—as it doubtless will for many readers.

I can't think of anyone who is better positioned to make all of these arguments and to have them heard than Patrick Shannon. His ideas are timely, important, powerful, and accessible and he writes with good humor and grace. He is a cultural and educational critic of the first order. But more than critiquing, he is also visionary. He walks his talk. He offers us a powerful alternative to the ways we often read, teach, and live—an alternative that is mindful of what we do (and could do) when we teach and read, of how we do it, and of what is ultimately at stake.

—Jeffrey D. Wilhelm, Boise State University;
Director of the Boise State Writing Project

Introduction: Why Do I Read?

This book is about reading as agency. More precisely, I describe my choices and actions as I learn to read the social things around me in order to accept them for what they are and also to consider why they are that way. I adopt a wide-awake, personal approach in order to demonstrate possibilities of reading in a world in which information appears to move at warp speed. I read those things as socially and historically constructed texts, which work to position me among competing social forces, telling me who I should be, what I should know, and what I should value. These thing/texts are not necessarily bad for me (or others), but they can be dangerous for some or all, if I (we) do not read them with those intentions in mind. In this way, my reading connects me with all other readers in a complicated daily activism of determining the main dangers we face. My personal choices and the negotiations of social choices are what make democracy possible and keep it vital. For educators, this could mean that our hopes for the potential roles for reading in our lives are tied to inquiries into our reading practices and the recognition that those practices domesticate as well as liberate us (and those we teach).

Are we fools? In his op-ed column in the *New York Times*, Frank Rich (2009) claimed that the most consistent narrative since the turn to the 21st century has been that Americans "have been so easily bamboozled." He pointed with embarrassment toward Enron, the invasion of Iraq, and the housing bubble. Heroes—Tiger Woods, John Edwards, and Bernie Madoff—proved to have feet of clay. Television fed us reality shows—*Survivor, Housewives of . . .* , and *American Idol*—without even a touch of reality. Experts supplied a constant stream of information celebrating each of these events, people, and entertainments, and then later explained why no one could have foreseen the clouds on the horizon. Rich argued that we foolishly consumed the celebrations and then endured the consequences. A few benefited wildly, while many suffered. He concluded that we're mired in this cycle with no obvious way out.

I'm not pessimistic about the present or the future. I don't think we are fools, ultimately. And I pin my hopes on reading. Not the reading that is discussed in newspaper headlines shouting about the high percentage of Americans that are illiterate, or the type that is taught in schools in order to pass state examinations. Those types limit our thoughts about *reading*, narrow the questions we ask about its possibilities, and impair our abilities to engage in civic life. Under those conditions, teaching reading becomes a means of production, which neither the student nor the teacher owns, and reading is considered human capital to be accumulated and then sold on the market to get a job. Such views of reading leave us as hamsters running in the wheel that Rich described. I'm searching for a definition of *reading* that will break that cycle, reclaiming the so-called illiterates and pushing me to realize that quality of civic life depends upon reading our way through the 21st century.

I want to read Rich's examples as if they were texts, understanding their promises and flaws in order to participate in the decisions that surround them. Those "texts" and too many others that I encounter attempt to separate me from decisions, telling me that I don't know enough to participate or discouraging me from asking too many questions. Perhaps this is what Rich meant by "bamboozled"—reading only to consume and follow. I seek reading that will enable me to participate as a citizen in a democracy, one who is connected to all other citizen readers. This book is a reflection on my approximations of that reading toward democracy across a broad sampling of texts. I admit that I am still learning to read like this. There, I said it. Although I'm a lapsed Catholic, at times, I still feel better after I confess.

I don't mean that I'm working on how to decode print, although I struggle to pronounce some names on the graduation list each semester. I am better than average at summarizing plots, directions, and arguments from a page. Rather, I'm learning how to employ these talents across new contexts and media in times that are changing more quickly than I can track. As I encounter more differences among readers and writers, I'm learning to recognize multiple readings of any text and to acknowledge that there are fewer grounds to assume that my reading is the correct one. As my ideas and contexts expand, reading becomes indistinguishable from what Charles Lemert calls "sociological competence," making sense of life in order to live it daily, and what C. Wright Mills labels "sociological imagination," the understanding that the personal always has social implications and connections. Lemert summarizes both in his book *Social Things*:

> To learn to live the sociological life is to learn to accept things as they come down, then to imagine why they are what they are. We live now in a time when life requires us to refrain from jumping too quickly to conclusions shaped by what we once believed to be true and good. (2008, p. x)

Although my English teacher, Mrs. Ennis, would circle Lemert's word *things* and write "vague" in the margin, Lemert chose *things* as a count noun in order to cover all affairs, concerns, ideas, and objects. Everything is social, he argues, touched by human choices and actions. Nothing built, private, or natural should escape our consideration, because all are influenced by the social. Lemert wants us to look at everything and think about why it comes to us in that form and what its consequences might be. Moreover, he cautions us to think slowly and deeply because some past stories that we've told ourselves about those consequences are neither accurate nor helpful to us or to others. We take a short step, it seems to me, if we think about Lemert's social things as "texts" that we read in order to negotiate our daily lives (social competence) and to connect our lives to those of others by thinking about possible and likely consequences (sociological imagination).

To demonstrate what I mean by reading toward democracy, I explain my readings of social things/texts from my everyday life. My examples are personal, and they cut across media (road signs, radio broadcasts, video games) and modes (print, photos, actions, talk, and gestures). This is a good place to acknowledge my limits and those of the book. Although I can bring a varied background of experience, thoughts, and values to bear, I am incomplete, even contradictory at times, within my efforts to read with sociological imagination. Some of what I bring comes from family. For example, my father was a labor organizer in the 1920s and 1930s, attending a week-long session with A. J. Muste at the Brookwood Labor College, and my mother was a curator of the Susan B. Anthony House for a time, as well as a docent for some archives holding Frederick Douglass's *The North Star*. At times, my father described his participation as "standing behind the little Jew to make sure that everyone signed a union card," and my mother would explain that Lenny Bruce's comic routine about the bigoted lending practices of a banker was about her stepfather. These and other stories rumble around in my head.

Some of what I bring is from my experiences. I've been a laborer, kindergarten teacher, sanding machine operator, insurance salesman, college professor, labor organizer, and test writer. I've been employed, unemployed, and underemployed; insured and uninsured; and a home-owner, renter, and freeloader. I've lived on a farm, in towns and in sub-urbs, as well as within cities of many sizes. I've always been White, heterosexual, and male, but for years I lived where I was among the ra-cial minority, and many people were sure I was gay when I told them I taught kindergarten and preschool. But I've never been really hungry, completely broke, or without hope for the future. I know that I speak from a relatively privileged position concerning race, class, and gender.

My agency as a reader is extended, but also limited as I shuffle among my past and present experiences, thoughts, and values in order to consider particular texts within specific contexts. Situated among so-cial things and the forces behind them, I do not, perhaps cannot, see all the connections that others with differing sets of experiences might rec-ognize clearly. This is not an excuse or an admission of lack of effort. Rather, I want to make clear that I will never match the imaginations of all readers who could and will make different choices about the main dangers among the texts I consider in the book. When readers make those connections and elaborations in the margins of this book, I hope they will share them with others and with me.

HERE WE GO

I live in a place nicknamed the Happy Valley, coined because the Penn-sylvania College (now Penn State University) kept the area relatively economically sound during the Great Depression. Spring Creek runs through the middle of the Valley and serves a variety of needs, from rec-reational fishing to a main water supply for the area. A small section of Spring Creek, the Canyon, has become an object of local debate because its current owner is about to sell, allowing speculation about its next transition. Discussions about the sale rest on multiple readings of the same section of Spring Creek. Each group of readers chooses to attend to a different set of symbols, different relationships among those symbols, and different narrative arcs in order to explain what the Canyon means and could mean to the community. Hikers describe the area as pristine, contrasting its native vegetation and rock formations with those of the surrounding developed areas. Local historians point to the thick forests, steady stream, and limestone that attracted Philip Benner and 100 iron-workers to the area in 1793. Anthropologists from the university identify 30 prehistoric sites in the Canyon with a "perfect recipe of natural landscape features that led to very long and high density occupation." A spokesman from the university administration (the most likely buyer) reports that the site requires forest, stream, and infrastructure maintenance in order to remain vital.

Each group reads the Canyon according to the hum of its daily life, and each produces texts about the Canyon that present different images, meanings, and futures for this place that is less than 5 miles from my house. Although I've never been there (you know, because of bugs and stuff), these secondary texts affect my life because each invites me and other community members to accept its expertise and to echo its positions. Of course, I could shrug and comment that I don't have an opinion, but then I am abandoning my community and neighbors. Although their readings of the Canyon/text overlap, the groups suggest different futures for the Canyon, and perhaps our community, because the Canyon is one volume in the library of struggles over land in the Happy Valley. To live in the Valley with social competence, I'm compelled to read the texts of the Canyon.

Reading the Canyon is complicated, however, by its relationships with the past, present, and future of the Happy Valley. For the past 100 years, the Canyon section of Spring Creek has been part of the Rockview State Prison grounds. Originally, it was part of a parcel intended to teach inmates to farm and feed themselves. Its current "pristine" state results from the 8-foot fence with barbed wire that sets a boundary between the inmates and the public. State legislators ordered its sale after I-99 bisected prison property, creating a security concern. In 1982, the Environmental Protection Agency declared Spring Creek a Superfund cleanup site after a factory upstream leaked "kepone" into the water. As a result, our town required a new water treatment plant and the fishers were subject to a catch-and-release policy. After a long community struggle, which I did not read, the university sold another former agricultural plot to local commercial developers. And not everyone is happy in the Valley, because unemployment and underemployment are on the rise here, too. Somewhere in the nexus of these relations lies the current meaning of the Canyon.

Perhaps in this example you can see why I confessed that I am still learning to read. To be a good citizen, I must engage the Canyon texts with social competence. By reading, I become aware of the local context in order to participate in the debate and decisions, come closer to other community members, and develop networks of meanings and social relationships that are useful now and could be useful in the future when reading other texts as well. But the Canyon texts are not just local and current, and therefore I must read with sociological imagination to develop some understanding of their relationships across time and place. Some of the texts reach back to before recorded history, and others connect the Creek with industrial and environmental policies around the world, dragging economics and politics to the center. In this way, reading our local debate links me with global discussions about land use and distribution, making our local issues representative of national and global problems as well.

I will argue in this book that any social thing/text has deep relationships that affect our lives in many, often unexplored, ways, and that reading is our primary means of exploration, leading to action. Although such reading might seem daunting, to refrain from it, it seems to me, would be dangerous in a democracy. I think this issue is behind Frank Rich's concern about Americans at the end of the 1st decade of the 21st century. If I don't read, who will do this reading for me? Who will decide the Canyon debate, the community land use, or the global negotiations of environments? Which positions will prevail? What stories will be told to legitimize those decisions and subsequent actions? Michel Foucault places this danger in context:

> My point is not that everything is bad, but that everything is dangerous, which is not exactly the same as bad. If everything is dangerous, then we always have something to do. So my position leads not to apathy, but to a hyper and pessimistic activism. I think that the ethico-political choice we have to make every day is to determine which is the main danger. (1983, pp. 231–232)

Rather, I think, than presenting an existential crisis—dangerous if you don't read and dangerous if you do—Foucault's hyper and pessimistic activism is a way to think about reading with social competence and sociological imagination. Social things/texts aren't bad, but they are dangerous because they always represent a past, present, and future that could influence our daily lives in particular ways. All readings of social things provide constructs, categories, taxonomies, priorities, hierarchies, measurements, practices, and justifications, influencing our interpretations and actions and leading us in particular directions that are dangerous—at least for some people. If we protect the Canyon's flora and fauna, then we won't provide the needed development to supply employment. If we make the Canyon a museum or an archeological dig, then neither hikers nor developers are happy. If we develop the land, then the fishers will likely have to return to catch-and-release. Someone's solution is someone else's danger. As more groups seek to be recognized in any community and across all communities, we must, as Lemert reminds us, acknowledge the dangers in the stories that we've told in order to legitimize decisions and actions in the past. If every thing and every reading is dangerous, we must be very careful in daily ethico-political choices.

Fundamental to that care is becoming sensitive to the power relationships among groups and their readings. Think about the mounds of data that the university can generate in service of its reading of the Canyon. Consider the university's access to the public through the media. Contrast that with the hikers' cameras, prose, and poetry and their access to the newspaper op-ed page and the Internet. These last tools are not meager, but they seem to be little match for those at the university's disposal. Being powerful or lacking power doesn't make a group's reading necessarily good or bad, but it makes it dangerous to some. If I want to consider many different Canyon texts, I must work harder to find some readings than I do others. Without making that effort to find the readings of the less powerful, however, I become susceptible to certain sets of dangers, to being bamboozled, in Rich's words, limiting my imagination about why things are as they are. I think that's what Lemert meant when he wrote, "We live in a time when life requires us to refrain from jumping too quickly to conclusions shaped by what we once believed to be true and good" (2008, p. x).

TENSIONS BETWEEN COMPETENCE AND IMAGINATION

Learning to read with social competence begins with infants and toddlers —children learn to read the social things around them so they may take their places in intimate environments—and never ends as our worlds expand. Consider my new neighbor Wade, who has just passed his 2nd birthday and is learning to read the differences between his and our home. His house is arranged for play—everything not meant for his touch is out of sight—and our house with children long gone is unprepared for the whirlwind that is Wade. On his second visit, however, Wade could already tell that he must act differently in the two environments in order to enjoy himself. Although his mother is ever vigilant, she has not articulated a set of rules explaining the difference. Rather, Wade watches our adult faces, as much as he listens, in order to live competently. This is a remarkable accomplishment for someone so young, and although articulate, Wade can't talk about his reading of these texts.

But clearly, Wade has readings of these environmental and human texts that order his world, as he picks up the wooden top and just looks at the porcelain piggy bank that my mother gave our daughter over 2 decades ago. In this way, the texts around him encourage him to fit into a frame of acceptable social competence. Because the texts are not perfectly aligned in both houses, and some are even contradictory, he has room to waver within, and test the limits of, this frame. If Wade failed to read those "correctly" for too long, however, we would worry about his normal social development.

Reading with social competence works across time and space, as nearly all people read their already existing social conditions, although those conditions vary widely, as do definitions of social competence. Each culture establishes its norms over time and expects its members to read its texts correctly, without the aid of obvious rulebooks or too much formal instruction. Many social institutions have arisen to reinforce those norms and to frame child and adult readings of social things. Schools, churches, political parties, hospitals, unions, professional organizations, even organized sports are designed to encourage particular readings, helping all to become socially competent group members. Continued misreadings make individuals subject to remediation, ranging from frowns, time-outs, and spankings to counseling, prison, exorcism, or stoning in order to keep all members reading on the same page.

To a point, reading from the same page is a valuable democratic goal because it saves citizens from rereading the same social things anew each day. In many cases, however, past decisions on the main dangers within societies that establish the normal habits of competence have not served all members well, justly, or equally. We have many historical and contemporary examples in which *normal* has been used as a tool and a weapon to protect privileged groups. Reading with social competence within these environments invites us to conform, even when many social things around us are inhospitable, even hostile. Reading to fit into hostile environments might be tactical, but it is not democratic. Moreover, because nonconformist readings are treated as personal deviations and are remediated as such, the nonconformist is discouraged from recognizing that others share his or her readings and from questioning the "hostile" social forms.

If we are to advance democracy, we need more than reading with social competence that leaves us with few ideas about our agency. We must develop our reading of social things to enable us to imagine how our personal troubles with historic and current definitions of normality and "the way things are" connect us directly with others who share our concerns. That is what I am trying to do daily—to read toward democracy by using my sociological imagination. There are obvious dangers around us with the environment in sharp decline, economies undercut by greed, natural resources in short supply and poorly distributed, and the mass production of wasted lives that threaten our lives and well-being. If Foucault is correct, and I think he is, then not just the obvious, but every social thing, is a potential danger to someone or some group. We cannot be apathetic and democratic simultaneously.

And so, I enter the Spring Creek Canyon debate recognizing the groups' consensus concerning the value of community betterment, but also identifying the dissensus among them on how that value should be defined. It's this consensus on values and dissensus on the definitions that make democracy in our community possible. The groups seek to define clearly their positions on community betterment in order to attract new members and build a coalition sufficiently large to win, or at least influence, the debate and subsequent action. My ethico-political choice among the positions of those groups, or ones I have yet to identify, will depend upon my consideration of which definition I judge to be the main danger in this context and at that time. To participate, I must use the tension between reading for social competence and my sociological imagination.

ABOUT THIS BOOK

I wrote this book as a narrative of self-discovery because I see myself at 60 to be a work in progress. I'm still trying to answer basic questions about my reading—what, why, how, when, where, and whether. To address those questions I've tried to follow a basic format for chapters. In all but the last chapter, I open with an italicized teaser, wondering about the meaning of the title, in order to set the concepts to be considered. In the body of the chapters, I rely on stories and current events in order to make the ideas about my reading more accessible. Those chapters end with brief sections on imagining pedagogy and reading theory, in order to keep a running commentary on those implications throughout the text. In the last chapter, I flip this order, beginning by reading theory and ending with a teaser about how I hope the ideas and practices described in the book might work once readers put the book down.

In Chapter 1, I describe a 13-hour road trip across half the United States as a means to demonstrate what I read and how those texts teach me in explicit and subtle ways. I discuss content, form, and intention concerning a variety of texts along the way. The chapter ends with pessimistic Rich-like conclusions about the cumulative effects of all those texts. Digging deeper into the question of how texts work on me, I consider issues of representation and practices of production in Chapter 2. I test my abilities to read with sociological imagination and to identify the dangers when the texts are bright and shiny and play to my interests and desires. I read the processes of production of Google Earth, the Little League Baseball World Series, and the Beatles, and I wonder how these texts mediate my thoughts about my relationships with others.

Chapter 3 addresses the question, How do I make sense of texts? challenging traditional views that either text or I am in control of meaning. I take up the practice of framing as a psychological and rhetorical strategy that discourages my thinking outside given parameters. By reading tropes such as *Too Big to Fail* and *A Nation at Risk*, and connecting them through their underlying discourse of the free market, I return to the issue of making ethico-political choices among competing positions. In Chapter 4, I admit that I don't own a dumb or smart cell phone, and attempt to bring my reading into the 21st century. Shift happens, but how is shift a social thing?

The last two chapters address the activism that Lemert, Mills, and Foucault recommend. Chapter 5 considers personal agency, starting by complicating my views on censorship. Am I for or against preemptive acts of stifling ideas in texts that I consider to be dangerous? My answer is yes. Moreover, I discuss how my convictions complicate my reading, testing whether or not I am able to read my hopes with a hyper and pessimistic activism. Can I accept what I propose as dangerous? In part, my decision to write this book is a result of those deliberations. In the last chapter, I pursue others reading sociologically in order to make ethico-political choices and to act on what they have identified as the main danger—the loss of democracy in their lives. To counteract that loss, they demonstrate personal and collective courage in the production of texts that represent sustainable communities in urban, suburban, and rural areas across Happy Valley; throughout the United States; and, using technology, around the world. Those texts offer multiple entry points to read toward democracy.

IMAGINING PEDAGOGY

I teach at a sore spot for reading education—where classroom teachers learn to work with students who struggle to learn to read at school. The psychological norms of my profession position this work as personal troubles—either the student or the teacher has a deficit. That is, neither has been able to fit the frame of acceptable social competence for his or her role. My job, then, is to correct the teacher according to those norms so that she or he can correct the students who struggle. Accordingly, if I were good at my job (my shot at competence), then we'd have few pedagogically incompetent teachers and fewer "abnormal" students. But student struggles persist despite over 100 years of scientific work in constructing those norms and billions of dollars devoted to enforcing them.

This is a social issue, not broad sets of personal troubles, with many texts to be read with sociological imagination. In the introductory class for "reading specialists," the teacher/students and I *historicize* the psychological norms, noting alternative conceptions of reading, curriculum, assessment, and pedagogy in academic texts, news media, and popular culture (watch Madonna teach Shirley Baker to read in the film *A League of Their Own*). We *identify* the demographics of which groups of students are represented as having personal troubles learning to read and consider the social issue of poverty (Berliner, 2009). In a later class on assessment, we *find* examples of how power and economic markets have worked and continue to work in order to promote psychological alternatives over other more sociological approaches (trace the commercial, scientific, and political life of Dynamic Indicators of Basic Early Literacy [DIBELS]). We *study* our independent learning of something new outside class and note the multiple ways that we enter that process and choose, use, and discard teachers of all types (check out my yoga warrior poses on YouTube—just kidding). We *examine* the same samples of students' work according to competing conceptions in order to anticipate the different consequences for students (read Kathy Hall's *Listening to Stephen Read* [2003]). And then, we *go* to Summer Reading Camp (a practicum and seminar).

At camp, the teachers join with a community artist in order to work with struggling elementary and middle school students in ways that demonstrate what they know and can do with text, challenging psychological norms for teaching and learning reading. Together they explore topics (toys, insects, maps) through a variety of texts (websites, textbooks, literature, comics, photographs, captions), in order to produce enabling (sketches, notes, models, stories, plans, descriptions) and performance texts (dramas, iMovies, museum displays, comic books, anthologies, webpages, webcasts). In this environment, teachers and students reposition themselves within reading education, addressing the social issues that constrain their work together in schools. Although none become revolutionaries set to overthrow the psychological norms, all participants change and will use their agency to alter their work at school in subtle, but profound, ways.

READING THEORY

With the phrase "We take a short step, it seems to me," I push reading to become a corollary of social theory—the accounts we articulate in order to explain what is going on around us and why it is that way. In *The Sociological Imagination* (Mills, 1959), I think I've identified a basic connection between the two—individuals can grasp relationships between their daily lives and social structures by recognizing the connections between their personal troubles and social issues. Although this idea can be located in the work of classical sociologists (Marx, Durkheim, and Weber), I've found more accessible portals. For example, Charlotte Perkins Gilman (in *The Yellow Wallpaper* [1887/1997]) wrote her way out of some patriarchal norms that assigned her to bed rest for wanting to work outside her household. Malcolm Little (in Malcolm X, *The Autobiography of Malcolm X* [1967/1987]) decided that racist social structures of schooling, employment, and housing were responsible, at least in part, for his incarceration. In *Rivethead* (1991), Ben Hamper described how the already disappearing General Motors assembly line in Flint, Michigan, accounted for his apparent lack of ambition in his personal life. More contemporary examples abound. Consider U.S. homeowners who have connected their inverted mortgages with unregulated banking practices (see, for example, Dustin Kidd's *Mortgages and Sociological Imagination* [2009]) or heavy poor people who've tapped the complicated nexus surrounding nutrition, wealth, food production and distribution, and obesity in the United States (for example, Sue Greer-Pitt's *Obesity and Air Conditioning* [2009]).

The norms of their times assigned middle-class White women to domestic lives, Black men to subservient status, working-class men to repetitive employment, and also mortgage holders to perpetual obligation and heavy people to social pariah status. And as Michel Foucault's *Civilization and Madness* (1961/1988) and *Birth of the Clinic* (1973) taught me as an undergraduate, the "help" offered to those who deviated from these norms is counseling, therapy, and rehabilitation, in order to bring them back to compliance. Each author recognized the limits of these assigned roles within the prevailing social structures and, somehow, found the courage to develop practical social theories, connecting "the larger historical scene in terms of its meaning for the inner life and the external career of a variety of individuals" (Mills, 1959, p. 5). Their agency began with the act of reading social texts (the wallpaper, the cell bars, the assembly line, debt, and grocery store shelves) in order to make that connection (their ethico-political choice about the main danger). As Bronwyn Davies argues, agency lies in "imagining not what is, but what might be" (2000, p. 67).

Before that reading connection was made, they operated within, and therefore reinforced, the norms and structures that seem to regulate their lives. The actions that followed were personal (deciding what to do) and social (finding others who've made a similar connection and choice after reading). There were few guarantees for outcomes, or even consistency, across readings and texts. It seems unlikely that these imaginative authors would read one another's texts and make the same connection or choose that connection as the main danger. To be honest, I'm not sure where I stand on walking away from debts incurred while speculating on house prices. Desire for predictability of reading, choices, and agency seems to me to be a longing for the grand narratives that Mills warned us about or the "jumping to conclusions shaped by what we once believed to be true and good" (2008, p. x) that Lemert included in his statement about competence and imagination. But that's just one more loose end in my learning.

CHAPTER 1

What Do I Read?

Fifty years ago, Vance Packard coined the term hidden persuaders to warn the public about the goals and tactics of ad men. His fears were that these men and their texts would teach us to consume their products, encouraging and creating desires by playing on our vulnerabilities. The main danger, he concluded, was that these men and texts would substitute consumerism for democracy as the center of American life. The troubles at the end of the 1st decade of the 21st century evince that Packard's prediction was not too far off its mark. His call to identify the hidden persuaders can be used to extend traditional notions of reading, text, and teaching beyond the classroom into our everyday lives and to focus our attention on what texts and pedagogies can do for and to us.

My summers are spent driving our kids to one place or another. It used to be short trips to lessons, sporting events, or friends' houses. Now it's to and from college campuses with all their stuff in tow or to and from internships in order to study the evolutionary genomics of corn or the contamination transport within differing ground systems. None of these activities can take place within 10 driving hours of our home. Each must be negotiated singly because they occur in opposite directions from one another. If one child goes to the Midwest, the other travels south or to the Northeast. As an aside, Kathleen and I (I'm married to Kathleen, although she often denies it) can't quite understand how two tragically hip reading teachers could raise a couple of science nerds, complete with plastic pocket protection from their pens.

At the end of the summer of 2006, I drove to Grinnell, Iowa, to deposit our daughter Laura for her senior year. Pointed west, we talked about her plans for that year and next, the curious fact that Indiana has outsourced its part of I-80 to a foreign company, and the inevitable truth that Chicago will never complete its can-of-worms road system in order to permit drivers to get where they want to go without swearing. On the drive back from Grinnell College, I listened to the radio, belting out oldies along with the station disc jockeys, eavesdropping on local talk shows, and paying attention to National Public Radio (NPR) in its various forms across two time zones. Within one 13-hour jaunt, texts of many sorts taught me four American lessons: to consume, to seek expert opinions, to romanticize the past, and to enjoy spectacle and celebrity. None of these lessons raises much hope for democracy.

DISCLOSURES

By recounting my reading of the texts on this road trip home, I hope to demonstrate reading with sociological imagination in order to employ Foucault's notion of hyperpessimistic activism of choosing the main dangers in my life. I understand my effort as an authentic example of everyday readings because many people drive and listen to the radio while thinking about what they hear, see, and do. This act of reading the social texts of everyday life, then, seems to be typical practice. I will argue that to read with sociological imagination is necessary for citizens to participate in the governing of their lives in a democracy—be it limited to what the golden arches mean, whether to vote for building that new school in your town, or how to understand such terms as *regime change* or *too big to fail*. My route to that goal has three stops along the way.

The first stop is the notion of public pedagogy—all institutions present lessons to us concerning what we should know, who we should be, and what we should value. They attempt to re-create us in their own image. They use specific pedagogical strategies that are not always readily apparent, but are nonetheless there, in the texts they produce. Think about churches, the police, and schools. Packard suggested that companies engage in public pedagogy through ads. Rich points toward media and think tanks. I think it's all of the above and more.

Second, I'll stop at the notion that the pedagogical strategies always involve texts, broadly defined, that are supposed to be read in particular ways. The texts during my drive were aural, visual, tactile, and even gustatory. That is, I listened to chatter, songs, and reports. I looked at the bumper stickers, lane dividers, and signs. I felt the ripple bumps before the ticket booths, the cold steel of the gas nozzle, and the hot tea (because my dad told me that coffee would stunt my growth). I tasted the sugar-laced foods in Iowa, Illinois, Indiana, and Pennsylvania and stopped for a salad in Ohio. I am happy to report that, although the steel plants are running to some capacity, I did not smell Gary, Indiana, as I used to when Kathleen and I worked at Purdue University, and we would drive to see the Cubs play at Wrigley Field. Regardless of their medium, each of these texts was organized through forms and conventions—they had a code to crack, a grammar to follow, meanings to construct, and intentions to discover. That is, they were organized to be read for social competence in order to teach us to live our daily lives in certain ways.

The third stop will be to acknowledge that pedagogies and texts always represent the ideological struggles to position me and to capture my allegiance. This was Packard's point about advertising—the texts and the people behind them are trying to sell us something—but all texts, not just ads, are out to get me. Although the texts are designed for more than me, I'll admit that I take them personally. I used to think that taking it personally was a problem, until I recognized that texts attempt to put others in similar positions as well. My individual issues were really social problems, and that, of course, is the beginning of using my sociological imagination while reading.

Think about my choice of radio network—at the time, NPR was on the second Bush administration's hit list because some government officials believed that the network projected a bias, trying to teach listeners to interpret their stories and the world the stories represented according to liberal values. And the Bush administration wasn't only concerned with the content of the news programs; it was also troubled by the ways in which NPR arranged its stories, the topics they selected and ignored, and the media they included. Perhaps we can readily examine the ideological slants between newspapers such as the *New York Times* and the *Wall Street Journal*; however, it might be more difficult to identify ideologies within texts of other institutions. Do you think of churches as ideological? Sports? Corporations? Museums? Schools? All are texts and produce subtexts that attempt to teach me who I should be, and that identity has a particular political view that corresponds with those text producers.

Because of this variation and the fact that these pedagogies, texts, and ideologies must rely on language to represent their meanings, their impacts are never complete or unitary. That is, they can't and don't convey uniform messages to or for all readers. Rather, the pedagogies and texts contain holes and contradictions that permit readers to insert themselves as active participants in order to negotiate possible meanings, identities, and relationships with others. Those holes and contradictions

make reading with sociological imagination possible. The acts of identifying contradictions, stepping into those gaps, and bending authors'
intentions are what Foucault meant by hyperpessimistic activism and
ethico-political choice about the main danger daily. To be active is to read
with sociological imagination, and I recognize that reading across media
requires different sets of practices that vary across time and place. That's
part of why learning to read has been a life project for me.

Using the texts of my journey home, I hope to demonstrate how social institutions (the government, courts, media, think tanks, businesses
big and small, sports, and even churches) use texts in order to re-present
the world for me and to teach me about my place within it. Each of these
institutions hides much of its intent to persuade. For example, throughout the day, I passed government traffic signs intended to regulate my
driving, positioning me and suggesting to me that I live in a society of
laws. The standardization of the signs and the articulation system among
signs (shapes, colors, symbol vs. alphabet) are intended to teach me that
I am a subject of the state, equal to all others. If this were not the expec-
tation of the authorities behind the signs, there would be qualifications.
And of course, there are some official qualifications marked on signs that
split speeds for trucks and cars, assign lanes only to carpools, and divert
only certain drivers to be weighed.

Do you see the public pedagogy within these texts? Standardization
of symbols and grammar were to represent equality and uniform expectations and to teach me that everyone will follow the traffic laws.
If we understand reading only as social competence in order to follow
lawmakers' intent for traffic signs, then we might be safe drivers, but we
would be baffled by what's really happening on the roads. The meaning
of these laws (all laws?) is negotiated continuously. By that I mean, no
one drove the speed limit, some never left the passing lane, and some
cars followed the trucks at the easy-on/easy-off rest stops instead of
complying with the signs/law segregating vehicles by size. To be sure,
patrol cars, hand signals, and wrecks mediated the negotiations of these
laws/signs/texts, but few followed the official readings of those traffic signs. Rather, most drivers interpreted the teaching of the signs because they understood that all signs convey more than is stated. How
many miles per hour can you drive above the speed limit without being
stopped for a ticket? The answer, of course, is contextual.

Exploration of that context reveals seamier sides to these negotiations. Despite the fact that the intentions of the standardization of

symbols are to convey a sense of uniformity and equality, standardization actually hides important realities of negotiations of what the signs mean. Minorities, teenagers, and the poor are more likely to be pulled over by the police; they are more likely to be ticketed and more likely to receive punishment—even more severe punishment than that of other groups of drivers. These realities are the social life of the texts/signs— how the signs work in society and for whom. Unless I read signs with sociological imagination in order to consider how the signs position me and others and what the signs hide, their standard format inhibits my recognition and evaluation of that social life.

Do you see? Without reading with sociological imagination, I am unable to decide on the main danger. The traffic signs help us live competently and safely, but they also limit us in ways that everyone negotiates. Those limitations are applied more directly and forcefully to some groups than others, and that seems dangerous in a democracy! My sociological reading doesn't suggest that I am advocating driving on the wrong side of the road. Rather, it identifies a contradiction between the appearance of the sign which signals that all are equal under the law and the fact that clearly we are not. The main danger for me in this example is that arbitrary enforcement of the law makes us all vulnerable.

READING WITH THE RADIO ON

One of the main NPR stories on the day of my trip home was U.S. district judge Anna Diggs Taylor's decision to halt the National Security Agency's warrantless wiretapping program that President Bush had authorized secretly in 2001. According to Judge Taylor, the president's program violated privacy and free speech rights guaranteed in the U.S. Constitution and the separation of powers among the three branches of government. She was quoted as writing (this is difficult to take down when you are driving):

> It was never the intent of the framers to give the president such
> unfettered control, particularly where his actions blatantly
> disregard the parameters clearly enumerated in the Bill of Rights.
> . . . There are no hereditary kings in America and no powers not
> created by the Constitution.

Clearly Judge Taylor's text is meant to teach us that the president overstepped the Constitution's intention to balance powers among branches of government in order to prevent the rise of a monarchy. The White House's immediate response was to say and repeat the phrase "national security during the War on Terror" as many times as possible. The administration hoped to substitute its text for Judge Taylor's by teaching us that *War on Terror* stands for the warrantless wiretapping, and therefore, legitimizes its use. The administration's statement/text was meant to teach listeners that we are at war, that it's a war against terror, and therefore the experts must take actions that are new and bold and outside the imaginations of the original framers.

For its part, NPR invited expert commentary to provide depth and to show its journalistic neutrality. Democrats applauded the ruling for the most part. Republicans spoke from a news release titled "Liberal Judge Backs Dems' Agenda to Weaken National Security." Anthony Romero, executive director of the American Civil Liberties Union, declared that Taylor's ruling was "another nail in the coffin" of the Bush administration's antiterrorism programs. In opposition, Bobby Chesney, a national security law specialist from Wake Forest University, stated, "No question that the ruling is a poorly reasoned decision." The political struggles are obvious.

But I want to draw your attention to NPR's practice of parading "experts" before the public in order to teach us that we have gained knowledge on the issues considered. NPR's practices of production can be treated as texts. In this case, listeners might ask: What is a national security law specialist or an expert? What does the category of *national security* entail? Why is a specialist or expert needed to understand this issue? How does NPR pick specialists or experts? Who picks them? What is the market for specialists or experts? How might that market have an effect on what can be said during a brief interview on NPR? These are critical questions left unaddressed on NPR that day, and perhaps, every other day as well.

As Packard argued about advertisers, institutions rarely make their intentions for their text completely explicit. Public pedagogies, then, and the texts they produce put the onus on the reader to construct the messages, purposes, and practices of production for themselves. With each new medium and new pedagogical strategy to teach us, readers must expand their repertoires of reading practices in order to determine the greatest dangers in their immediate and future contexts. No text is neutral, and readers are never safe from public pedagogy or ideology.

Billboards, on nearly every mile of the highway, act as the Sirens did for Odysseus. "Stop to fill up," they inveigle. Fill up in every way imaginable. The signs compete with each other near (with several alternatives listed on one sign) and far (as some invite you to drive past the closest businesses in order to stop at ones distant and more exotic). The signs don't just inform; they create as well. As I drove along I-80, I felt—not just thought, but felt—that I could use a discount pair of pants or shoes, a Krispy Kreme doughnut, or fireworks! Some signs worked simply from branding. Their logos alone evoked the visions in my head that companies worked so hard to create over time. Packard made this point in the 1960s, and Naomi Klein updated it not so long ago in *No Logo*.

The green circle with the white queen of beans invited me for a venti chocolate macchiato half decaf, low fat with whip for way too much money, and the pink double Ds inveigled me to stop for a sugar ring donut. Sometimes logos work strangely over time. In our family's early driving trips, the golden arches meant clean, or at least cleaner, restrooms with changing tables. That story remains clearly in my head to this day. When I see the arches now, I always steer clear. Those days are over—I'm only somewhat happy to say.

Branding and logos seek to position the reader as the lead in a story of ownership and consumption. In that order, thank you. Buy, then consume, and then buy again. Just as Aldous Huxley envisioned in *Brave New World*—"End not mend" was the official slogan delivered through hypnopedia (one of my favorite terms). This type of storying began with the randy behaviorist John B. Watson after he left academia for Madison Avenue in 1921. Thank Watson for the piles of goodies next to the cash registers in grocery stores, because he said, "Like rats in the maze, consumers reach for the items within proximity." In 1923, Watson invented program lead-ins to advertising when he delivered a 10-minute national radio lecture on the glands that he ended at the mouth, just before his sponsor's commercial for toothpaste. After his empirical tests demonstrated that consumers could not identify their favorite brands by senses alone, Watson proposed that Americans "walk a mile for a Camel," "take a coffee break with Maxwell House," and follow the advice of the queens of Spain and Romania to use Ponds cold and vanishing cream. In each of these "stories," the reader was to see him- or herself with the hip, new ways of living and, of course, buy the product. We have not come a long way baby from Watson's invention of market research.

Logos and slogans are supposed to evoke the appropriate story with the least amount of institutional exposure. That happens just as Watson planned, with the text becoming the stimulus and the pleasant story association resulting as the conditioned response. The Stimulus-Response (S-R) chain continues with the story leading directly to purchases. The pedagogical strategy of repetition of the stimulus-and-response connections works dramatically as we open our wallets to satisfy immediately our desires created and fulfilled by business. Advertisers are particularly adept at this stimulus-and-response strategy because they can part a fool and his money—sometimes lots of money—in 30 seconds or less. Buyer beware!

Another NPR story during my trip home that summer demonstrated just how wary a buyer must be. U.S. district judge Gladys Kessler ended a 7-year federal case against tobacco companies by agreeing that for 50 years the tobacco CEOs had conspired to deceive the public about the health risks of smoking. The judge ordered the companies to apologize publicly, admit their conspiracy to deceive, and stop trying to teach the public that the hazards of smoking are abated with "light, low tar, mild, or natural cigarettes." These terms were used to fool the public about what the companies had known since 1954, when CEOs met at a New York hotel to agree to the cover-up. The judge described tobacco as a "highly addictive product that leads to a staggering number of deaths per year, an immeasurable amount of human suffering and economic loss and a profound burden on our national health care system."

Again NPR trotted out experts to demonstrate the network's legitimacy. The experts presented a couple of sides to the story. William Corr, the executive director of the Campaign for Tobacco-Free Kids, applauded. Mark Smith, an R. J. Reynolds spokesman, stated, "We're gratified that the court did not award unjustified and extraordinarily expensive monetary penalties, but we're disappointed that Kessler found the firms had engaged in conspiracy." Again the expert opinion is a wash, and dare I say uselessly predictable. No expert on NPR mentioned anything about the fact that the prosecuting federal government actually subsidizes tobacco production through the Department of Agriculture, that antismoking education has been effective only with middle-class and White segments of the U.S. population, and that the required public apologies would bring smoking to the public's attention and therefore promote it. Although none of these opinions were heard on NPR, each was voiced within a 2-minute segment on a CBC broadcast from Windsor, Ontario, that I caught while rolling past Toledo.

In this example, I encountered the market ideology that brings much of the American right and left political ideologies together in the celebration of capitalism and its right to direct modern, and even postmodern, life. The "free market" worked for 50 years, to the misery of millions of people and a cost of billions (an estimated $280 billion in company profits and medical costs of hundred of millions). Without effective government regulation, even with government support, captains of industry and those who worked for them put profit above people's well-being. The texts of tobacco companies hid this message and these connections, which should cause readers concern about the dangers of oil companies, mortgage lenders, the processed food and pharmaceutical industries, and Wall Street firms, to name the obvious.

Without a subscription channel to carry me across the country, I had to punch the scan button to maintain constant aural stimulation. That act brought two distinct, but somewhat overlapping, voices to my ears. Oldies-but-goodies DJs and Christian preachers seem to rule the airwaves between central Iowa and central Pennsylvania. They are particularly crowded around the 80s and 90s numbers on the radio "dial"— often in competition with public stations. I don't want to get in too much trouble here, so I will tread softly.

First, let me say that oldies aren't as old as they used to be. Kurt Cobain and Nirvana do not perform oldies—despite what some disc jockeys tell you. Dion and the Belmonts perform oldies. "Well I'm the type a guy, who likes to roam around" are lyrics to the perfect song for driving home. As I listened to oldies, my rented Hyundai became my parents' Ford 300, and I forgot my present and invoked the past. Each song invited me to forget the day's events—29 killed in Baghdad, France balking at leading a peacekeeping force in Lebanon—and remember the glories of my youth. Then, life was simple. Shoo doop be do be do, shoo doop be do be do.

Nostalgia is potent. Conservatives hold it as a core value. If the present were like the past, things would be better, they say, without much evidence. Well, my 1950s had American-enforced regime changes as well—perhaps you remember Iran in 1953 and Guatemala in 1954—one for oil and the other for food. My 1960s had American-enforced regime changes in Vietnam (South, not North) and my 1970s had Chile. You get the picture, and remember that those pictures of nostalgia are always air-brushed. Spun in whatever direction the text maker wants to take you. The pedagogies surrounding nostalgia have the same intention as the magician who points in one direction to hide what she's doing with the other hand. Nostalgia has been powerful politically. Think "Morning in America" (President Reagan's campaign theme and still the title of William Bennett's non-NPR talk radio show). It works economically as well because it delivers a certain demographic. Perhaps that's why station disc jockeys now date their oldies period for their stations—the best of the 1970s, 1980s, and 1990s—and my era gets played only before dawn, when men my age have to get up to pee.

Radio ministers evoke nostalgia as well—"Gimme that old-time religion." They teach reading directly on their broadcasts. That is, they name, read, and explain scripture to an audience to save them from a horrid afterlife. Reading reveals God's words, and those words solve the teleological puzzle of human life by giving it purpose. We are here, they say, to prepare to live eternally with God's grace. But life on earth is tempting and confusing, and radio ministers help listeners address those temptations and confusions by naming them and locating scripture that provides answers. Because those answers are not transparent, ministers mediate them and speak for God. That's a pretty strong authority—even to a lapsed Catholic like me. They treat text as if it were closed, with a single meaning. Not a meaning reached through negotiation, and then consensus, mind you, but one that identifies truth. We ignore this revealed truth at our peril.

Although comforting, I'm sure, this is a bad reading lesson because texts do not have single obvious meanings. Rather, readers construct meaning from texts—even the Bible. If that were not true, there would be no need for ministers or different Christian sects, because the Bible would transfer God's meaning directly. But biblical scholars and lay readers continue to pore over that text to find new meanings. As a first-generation American of Irish descent, I know that there are disputes over God's truth, and ministers and priests can differ on the meaning of scripture—the word of God—leaving us with multiple gods speaking multiple truths depending on which point on the dial we select. And these differing gods have differing amounts of power behind their authority as national ministries on the airwaves and through cable networks compete with local mega-churches, town congregations, and small sects across the nation.

Trying to understand how multiple gods and multiple truths are possible is overwhelming and often sorrowful. But even among radio stations the problem is clearly before us. And beyond the radio airwaves that day, Lebanon and Israel had just agreed to a ceasefire and Baghdad was still burning. The problems posed by multiple god authorities and multiple truths are clearly reading issues with multiple texts, many pedagogical strategies, and several ideologies. Dig in at your own risk.

Through the legislation No Child Left Behind (NCLB) and the Education Science Reform Act of 2002, the federal government named science as Truth in the reading field. According to these texts, the nation can be certain that all citizens will become readers, if they are taught according to scientifically based methods. I found it interesting, then, when NPR reported during my drive home that after 7 decades of measurement and testing, scientists were preparing to vote in order to determine if Pluto were to remain a planet. What a great lesson in how language works to change truth and reality to whatever we want it to be. Clarify the definition, vote on truth, and, poof, Pluto is gone as a planet. The NPR story revealed science for what it is, BOGSAT—a Bunch of Guys Sitting Around a Table making decisions based on criteria that they deem to be important. (Our daughter, whom I dropped off at Grinnell during this trip, objects to this characterization. Although she accepts the critique of the rhetorical basis of science as reasonable, she challenges the word *guys*—as she makes room for her seat at that table while studying evolutionary genetics of plant domestication.)

This example might seem silly because it doesn't appear to harm anyone except the poor schmuck stuck with a warehouse full of nine-planet mobiles. When we think about the practice of BOGSAT, determining definitions and goals, and measuring truth accordingly, then we might identify dangers. Consider the multiple definitions of reading proficiency levels for school children under NCLB in each of the 50 states. In 2006 when I was driving, each state set its standards and method of measurement in order to determine whether or not students were proficient as readers. Because of the different standards and different measures, students could change their status as readers simply by stepping across state lines. To put state scores in perspective, the Bush administration required states to use the National Assessment of Educational Progress (NAEP) as a national measure of proficiency. To date, the differences between state tests and the NAEP are considerable, with some state tests showing three times as many students to be proficient in reading as the

NAEP test. Of course, NAEP is a product of a different BOGSAT. Poof, some students are gone as proficient readers.

Two stories occupied most of the airtime on NPR and other news networks during my drive. The first story announced the arrest of a suspect in the JonBenet Ramsey case. The second speculated that Tiger Woods was well on his way to winning a 12th major golf tournament. As you might remember, JonBenet Ramsey was a 6-year-old child beauty queen who was murdered on the day after Christmas in 1996. Perhaps you recall the case and the years of tabloid reporting that followed. The new suspect was arrested while teaching second grade at a private school in Bangkok, and he was to be extradited to Colorado within a week. Sound bites from Mr. Ramsey, two other relatives, the Colorado district attorney, three FBI officials, and a homeland security officer were aired throughout the day as the story grew in size, if not importance. In effect, the story became inescapable. This event grew to extreme proportions in the weeks that followed, only in the end to be exposed as a hoax through genetic forensics.

This is spectacle, and it works in two ways. First, multiple texts create desires around the way in which the well-to-do and famous live. They have multiple homes, expensive tastes, and interesting lives, and we do not. They have it easy or appear to have it easy, and we don't. We should envy them for what they have. When something happens to them, their lives become open for inspection and their problems seem all the more tragic. We worry for their families as if they were the only ones to suffer such blows. Second, the texts of spectacle are often to be read as a morality play in which the ways that these others live are scrutinized and judged. Here, the simple life becomes valorized because it does not lead to the moral decadence that swirls around and within the famous. The tension between these two parts of spectacle can be overwhelming because we feel bad for the murder of the child, but appalled by the revelations of her exploitation as a sexual object at 6. With each new element, the twists and turns become overwhelming as more and more media texts move into the market to create, maintain, and feed our voyeuristic needs.

Tiger Woods is the Mozart of our times—a child prodigy whose father paraded him on the *Mike Douglas Show* at 3 in order to show off his swing and perform tricks. Now in his 30s, Woods is arguably the best golfer ever. On the first day of the PGA Championship in 2006, even before Tiger hit his first ball, the news was full of the possibility that he could win that tournament. Excuse me, but on the 1st day isn't it possible for any participant to win—at least theoretically? It's premature for the story on victory before the event happens, but there are entire sections of newspapers, websites, journals, and even television networks devoted to such speculation on sports.

Sports stories are to teach us about the scoreboard of life. Winners get attention and applause because sports competitions are metaphors for survival. In these texts, practice always pays off. Poise is required. Any barriers can be overcome. "Work hard," they teach, "and you'll be a winner." Sports texts don't relate that the "loser" practiced often as well. Many people who do not make it to the tournament practice hard. But on the scoreboard and the talk around it, the rest of the pack just doesn't have it—even though they make terrific livings hitting balls and walking over hills and dales.

At the time, Tiger Woods was a celebrity and just damn fun to watch and read about. He allowed cameras into his house to sell Buicks and watches and whatever. He traveled to Dubai just to hit golf balls into the ocean off the world's most expensive hotel island. Behind his celebrity were his golf abilities, and he stayed a bright celebrity because he won (until it was discovered that the created image was not the reality). Other celebrities, however, are famous for being famous. Consider the family that lost on a reality television show and then created the hoax of their son floating away in a hot air balloon. All the stories and infotainment that surround them teach us what can happen in the United States. If you become a celebrity, you can become rich and "party like it's 1999." Play golf, confess murder, or become the American Idol, it's all the same. Once you get the public eye, you have it made.

The JonBenet and Tiger stories occupied the news like a siege as I drove home. During the early hours of the day, these stories were small, but as the day wore on (13 hours, remember) these stories overwhelmed the rest of the news. The ubiquity of these texts set the day's agenda for drivers. I was going to relive spectacle and celebrity through true crime and sports, and try as NPR might, the two verdicts—can you remember them at all after our 15 minutes of fame with JonBenet and Tiger?—were pale in comparison, although each had direct consequences for every listener's life. You don't have to be a fan of Paddy Cheyefsky and Sidney Lumet's vision of news in the film *Network* to understand the direction of this agenda. Crime, celebrity, and sports are the topics that keep an audience.

LESSONS TAUGHT

As I crossed the Ohio-Pennsylvania border between Youngstown and Sharon, the overall lessons of the texts of my day dawned on me. First, I think that it is clear that it's not just advertisers who engage in public pedagogy, seeking to teach us what we should know, who we should be, and what we should value. The government, business, media news and entertainment, church, science, sports, and other institutions are texts and use texts in order to position us according to their intended goals. As the texts from my daylong drive demonstrated, these institutional goals were all political but were not all aligned or even consistent. For example, federal officials prosecuted and funded the tobacco industry, and some continue to smoke. Business creates desires, fulfills needs, and resists regulation. Science claims objectivity, but voted to discontinue a scientific "fact." Within such texts, readers with sociological imaginations can insert themselves in order to decide which are the main dangers for their lives and perhaps the lives of others around them.

For me, the main danger of the texts of my trip was the fairly uniform lesson that positioned me as a consumer. Over the roadways and airwaves, institutions' texts taught me not only to consume goods and services, but also to swallow expert opinion, idealized representations of the past, and the spectacle of celebrity and success, as if these social things were representations of the way things are and should be. Each taught that I was to receive from others rather than create for myself, and that I was free to choose among goods, services, or ideas that institutions presented to me. I could choose a Krispy Kreme or a Dunkin' Donut, a Republican or a Democrat, and faith or science. Little space was created for me to think outside these parameters or to consider what had been left unstated in the texts. The steady diet—even from public radio—obscured the dangers for both my agency and my identity. Call me Consumer.

The text taught me to listen and learn, but not to think and act. Don't worry about business excesses, because the courts will take care of them. Don't fret about world issues or government intrusions into private lives, because there is balance among powers. Don't be anxious about the future, because experts have it all planned. Never mind about any of this, because a better world awaits believers, and after all, the Yankees could win the series this year. These texts asked me to turn away from civic life because I'm not smart enough to understand and to seek only comfort and security for myself.

Let me tell you, it's a long way from the border to the exact center of Pennsylvania, where I live, with those lessons spinning in my thoughts. It's particularly troublesome if you teach reading for a living, as I do, and you believe that a literate citizenry is a foundation for democracy. Currently the official school curriculum for reading emphasizes reading for social competence in order to help young citizens find their ways economically into the emerging social norms of the 21st century. If done well, reading for social competence could help many students to fit in to that society. Yet, as the texts of my drive taught me, our society is still fraught with the dangers of inequality and injustice, and it still promotes consumption over participation in civic life in ways that Packard would recognize after 60 years.

IMAGINING PEDAGOGY

"We Are . . . Penn State." That's one of the rallying cries that organize our student body into a collective group. At sporting events, one section of the crowd offers the call, and then another supplies the response. Between cheers for the Philadelphia Eagles and the Pittsburgh Steelers on the drunk bus that students ride "home" from bars and parties late at night, I am told that someone will unite the two groups by calling, "We Are." Even when frustrated by the university's bureaucracy, some wag will respond with an ironic "We Are" (skip a beat) "Penn State." The chant accomplishes more than a declaration of group solidarity, because the brand, Penn State, stands for a host of values: academic excellence, scientific research, mission to the state, status among international institutions, the dance marathon, Joe Paterno, and parties (we are number 1!).

Each semester, I attempt to have my undergraduate elementary education majors stretch their thoughts about public pedagogy, text, ideology, and positioning theory by reading Penn State college apparel. Like that chant, Penn State apparel signifies school spirit and commitment to university values. Everyone admits to having at least one article of Penn State apparel and many wear an example to class. I ask the students to read the messages on Penn State apparel in order to consider what the university and wearer intend to communicate. Although the letters and symbols on the apparel differ, the students seem clear that the apparel is a text that functions as public pedagogy, positioning all as aligned with at least some aspect of the university's ideology about itself. And for the most part, these students are eager to assent to that position—after all, we are Penn State.

They are not so keen, however, when we read the university's and their position with more sociological imagination. Virtually all Penn State apparel is made through a complicated system of subcontractors, who pay workers poorly, work them long hours, and provide few benefits. Some students call these sweatshop conditions, but university officials explain that Penn State apparel is made according to industry standards monitored by an industry-sponsored organization. Descriptions of the working conditions that the students read and observe on the Internet disturb many of them, and the students acknowledge that this new information changes their relationship with the university. Now when they wear or see the apparel, they read more than the university's intended message and comprehend "We are Penn State, and we condone appalling labor practices abroad."

This exercise is intended to elicit the same feelings that I had when I crossed the state line on my drive home. Call us consumers. In this case, we buy the apparel (yes, I have a Penn State sweatshirt), the university's ideology, and the market message that industry will police its labor practices without regulation. To avoid the equivalent to that lonely last 2 hours from the state line to my house, we talk about agency. What are our options for personal action, if this example is a metaphor for a structure that drives our lives? That question with this example has multiple entry points, and students use many of them—join United Students Against Sweatshops, reconsider the imprint of our consumption locally and around the world, teach others about the issue, investigate teachers' collective bargaining, wear the apparel inside out, question education as the consumption of information, and many others. . . .

READING THEORY

I spent so little time on public pedagogy in the chapter because the concept seems so obvious to me—there is a great deal of teaching that happens outside school classrooms in public (as well as private) spaces. Similar to in-school pedagogy (Simon, 1992), public pedagogy attends to matters of curriculum in design and content, its strategic or tactical delivery, as well as evaluation. It poses a particular political vision of who we are and what our places are in the workings of the world. Archeologists find artifacts of public pedagogy in buried ruins (consider the multiple interpretations of cave paintings, e.g., Curtis, *The Cave Painters*, 2006) and anthropologists note diverse forms of public pedagogy across sites in the construction of cultures. The *Handbook of Public Pedagogy* (Sandlin, Schultz, & Burdick, 2009) defines public pedagogies as spaces, sites, and languages of culture that maintain dominant practices while also offering room for critique and reimagination—all of which is essential to the construction and negotiation of identities and social formations.

To maintain, critique, reimagine, construct, and negotiate, agents design and create texts to signify their intentions for themselves and others to read with competence. While these texts do not carry the authority to ensure that intentions will be realized (as Lacan, 1968, told us, words take on new significance, threats, power, and desire for each person as they circulate), each text becomes "something like an arena in which reader and author participate in a game of the imagination" (Iser, 1974, p. 275), with text structures setting parameters for their expected readings. My favorite image of an explanation of this arena comes from Dinita Smith's (1998) interview with Jacques Derrida in which she describes him as standing and waving his arms around a New York City restaurant, exclaiming that "everything is text." Smith read Derrida's gesture as naming all people, objects, and actions in and outside the restaurant as "readable" texts. Perhaps, readers might not be privy to the immediate social and historical codes of the textuality of folded napkins, the subtle actions among intimate couples flirting across tables, or nuanced presentations of the foods on the plate, and so on; however, we can read each competently enough as readerly texts to fit in and, with effort perhaps, read them with sociological imagination as writerly texts (Barthes, 1982).

To paraphrase Bakhtin (1990) and Voloshinov (1973), every text is ideological. Whenever and wherever a text is present, ideology is present. Ideology can refer to "a system of belief common to a particular group," "a system of illusory beliefs," or "a general process of the production of meanings and ideas" (Williams, 1977, p. 55). In this way, texts are not the sole construction of individual authors, but rather act as markers for groups' explanations of the world and the appropriate deeds, habits, and institutions that make it run. The ideology precedes the texts and is influenced, in turn, by the societal effects of those texts. Texts, then, are a form of public pedagogy that operate imperfectly, seeking to maintain or challenge dominant practices and values as if they were common sense, normal, natural, and right.

The public pedagogies of texts weave stories that offer readers positions within their ideological narratives. When considered singly and continuously, most of the texts of my trip offered me various positions as a consumer (of expert opinion, goods, services, God's word, myths of government and economic rationality, etc.), preparing me to adopt a unified knowable identity as a competent individual who has made my mind up to define myself by counting my acquisitions of ideas, values, behaviors, and things, and eventually by asking that my consumer identity be acknowledged by others through credentials, affiliations, and status. According to Bronwyn Davies and Rom Harre (1990), the imprecision of language, the incomplete openness of text, and the constructive nature of relationships between pedagogy and learning afford readers choices among the competing, often contradictory, ideological intended selves to be produced. Perhaps the easiest contradictions to identify among the collective stories of my trip are the ads for products and the court decision about tobacco companies, the religious interpretations and decisions about Pluto, and the nostalgia of oldies and the current events of NPR. My recognition of those spaces of contradiction and the different positions available to me inside and outside the texts make room for ethico-political choices about the main danger and the agency of creating countertexts to disrupt intended norms.

CHAPTER 2

How Do Texts Work on Me?

Although I should know better, I still approach many texts innocently as if they were somehow outcomes of natural processes that help me understand the essence of social things. Without thinking, I believe that the newspaper describes events, shiny apples at the store are fresh, and Jesus loves me. It's a struggle for me to keep in mind while reading that every text (including the Spring Creek Canyon) is artificial—affected by human thoughts and actions. I know that there are parts of the ocean floor that have yet to be explored, but I'll bet there are empty Budweiser cans there. To read with sociological imagination is to recognize that all texts are the products of processes of production in which individuals and groups make specific decisions regarding every symbol, grammar, and design, which influence how we, and our students, might see ourselves and the world differently.

Our son, Tim Pat, majored in geography in college. It's a broad interdisciplinary field that enabled him to indulge his interests in science and politics in ways that neither of those separate fields embrace—at least on his campus. To have topics of conversation beyond his evening plans when he came home for visits, I started to study something about geography. I hoped to appear interested, if not smart, across the dinner table. My first association with geography was maps, texts that I used frequently when I drove him and my daughter Laura across the country to college and internships. Those Rand McNally road atlases were my salvation at times, and then were a source of cursing when our destination fell in a spiral binding or behind a staple on the older versions.

Unlike my road atlas, the earth is round. One challenge for any cartographer is to represent that shape on a flat surface. Many have tried, and each attempt is relatively dangerous according to a reader's point of view. These dangers began with the first sketchy renderings and continue with the digital signals that become photographic images sent from satellites. None can capture the truth or reality of the Earth's shape completely, because cartographers compose them from a point of view, which directs their decisions of what to include and how to include it—all of which is captured in the symbols and organization of the map/text. Consider the first world maps, which peeled the top and bottom of a globe in order to make a cylindrical map and then cut that shape to obtain a flat surface. These projections maintained relatively accurate shapes for landmasses, but distorted their relative sizes. Landmasses closer to the poles appear larger on the cut cylinders, and those at the equator seem condensed. On the Mercator version from the 16th century, Greenland appears to be the same size as Africa, although the large island is only 8% of Africa's actual size. The danger, of course, comes with a map's influence on our perceptions of the world.

The Mercator map was developed as a navigational tool that enabled ship captains to draw a straight line between launch and landing in order to determine the proper points on the compass to follow. It worked and works well for that function. Although it was not meant to be a useful representation of the earth's land surfaces, it became the projection selected for use in most school textbooks and popular magazines in Europe and North America. In 1902, geographers warned that "people's ideas of geography are not founded on actual facts, but on Mercator's map" (as quoted in Monmonier, 1994, p. 21). In 1947, the *Scientific Monthly* stated that the "use of the Mercator projection should be adjured by authors and publishers for all purposes" (Boggs, 1947, p. 470). Its continued use and efforts to confront its biases, however, forced the National Geographic Society in 1989 to call for a ban on all rectangular regular coordinate maps because "world maps have a powerful and lasting effect on peoples' impressions . . . [and] frequently seeing a greatly distorted map tends to make it 'look right,' . . . [and] such maps promote serious erroneous conceptions" (as quoted in Robinson, 1990, p. 101). In 1998, the National Geographic Society endorsed the Winkel Tripel projection that uses mathematical formulas to represent the curved nature of the earth upon a flat surface with "very small distance errors, small combinations of ellipticity and area errors, and the smallest skewness of any map" (Kessler, 2000, p. 29).

Yet even that projection continues to place the Northern Hemisphere at the top of the world; North America at the upper-left-hand corner of the map, where those literate in Latin or Cyrillic scripts are most likely to gaze first; and Europe at the top center. Tim Pat tells me that there is no fixed orientation in space in which our North Pole would always be on top. Although I find this a bit frightening, I remember the famous photo of the earth from Apollo 17 that had the South Pole at the top and Madagascar at the center of the globe. When it was first released, NASA flipped that photo in order to make the land shapes more recognizable to the general public. When we use a map turned "upside down" with the labeling of countries flipped as well, our undergraduate students turn the map around to "the right way" and are willing to read the countries' names upside down in order to locate destinations. Perhaps it's just habit that drives their decision to read the print symbols upside down rather than to look at the world differently, but there seems to be a contradiction between their comfort with different symbols being presented as right or wrong.

The development of digital tools for representing physical geography changes the way we think about ourselves and our place in the world. Digital tools give the impression of capturing the reality of places on earth in neutral and objective images. It appears that we are there, experiencing the landscapes as they exist without the mediation of others. Although cartographers at Google Earth use a different medium from that of paper, they still construct these maps. Such images are photographs, which as anyone with a driver's license knows do not always show it like it is. There are many elements to consider when thinking about any photographic representation—point of view, lighting and shadows, moment in time, power of a lens, and talent of the photographer (and my barber). Photographers' choices on these matters can precede the shot and then can also be reconsidered during the "developing." The Google Earth cartographers choose among possible photographs of an area and sometimes blend photographs together in order to obtain the highest quality, accounting for timeliness, resolution, cloud cover, light conditions, and color balancing.

Here's what I mean. Within 24 hours of Hurricane Katrina, amateurs began to fly low over New Orleans in order to take photographs of the damage. Google Earth made some of these images available almost immediately, helping evacuees and interested citizens understand what had happened to public and private property. Within a year, however, Google Earth reverted to pre-Katrina pictures of New Orleans. Brad Miller, the Democratic chairman of the House Committee on Science and Technology's Subcommittee on Investigations and Oversight, wrote a letter of inquiry to Google Earth, stating, "The entire country knows that New Orleans is a great American city struggling to recover from an unprecedented disaster. Google's use of old imagery appears to be doing the victims of Hurricane Katrina a great injustice by airbrushing history" (2007). Maps/local/earth director of Google Earth, John Hanke, responded, "Our goal throughout has been to produce a global earth database of the best quality" (as quoted in Broache, 2007). The pre-Katrina aerial photography was of much higher resolution than the amateur photos, but they were poor representations of the earth on which New Orleans was built, destroyed and now reconstructed in part. The replacements represented neither physical New Orleans at that time nor the efforts to bring the city back in a different image from what was then under way. For some reason, someone or someones decided that higher resolution trumped timeliness for the representation of New Orleans on Google Earth.

In this example, the process of cartography is exposed, at least a little. Cartographers make decisions about which criteria they will feature based on social conditions in which they work. At one point, timeliness seemed most important/useful/appropriate, and then later, resolution became more compelling. Why and how this happened is a matter for further research, but the choice about representation is clear. Reading these Google Earth maps of New Orleans for social competence enables you to make decisions about your relationship with that space, its past, present and future, and with the people who inhabited, inhabit, and could inhabit New Orleans according to the decisions made by the mapmakers. Such reading makes the text work accordingly to meet readers' purposes only within the parameters established in the practices of production. The maps aren't just objects to be read with social competence. They are also processes of production, which when read with sociological imagination make visible the decisions concerning representations of reality.

Reading the maps as objects only is dangerous, it seems to me, when it occludes access to the conditions of cartographic practices of production. And as the geographers acknowledged with the Mercator projections, maps mediate intentionally our understandings of relationships with other people. What and who are to be considered important, near, or similar are represented in the lines, shapes, colors, and orientations of the maps. Reading the maps with sociological imagination requires that I push past the graphic representations in order to discover the subjective, decision-making nature of the process of cartography. Representative Miller implied that Google Earth's decision to revert to pre-Katrina data was politically motivated, and Director Hanke argued that it was simply a matter of scientific quality control. Both can be correct, of course—wouldn't the decision to put the amateur photographs of post-Katrina be a political decision as well, involving some concern for quality? Either claim or all the ones that might be made between those parameters are within the conditions surrounding the practice of making maps and any other representational text, its public pedagogy, and its intended ideology.

WHERE HAVE YOU GONE, JOE DIMAGGIO?

Just up the road from the Happy Valley in 1939, Carl Stoltz organized his three nephews and their neighborhood friends into two teams to play baseball in a vacant lot in Williamsport, Pennsylvania. They experimented with field dimensions through that summer, and then Stoltz announced his league open for sponsorship of three teams. Jumbo Pretzels, Lundy Lumber, and Lycoming Dairy were the first businesses to field Little League teams. Currently, there are over 220,000 sanctioned Little League programs in 80 countries around the world. In addition, there are softball teams for girls and a challenge league for youths with physical disabilities. Players are assigned to leagues by age, beginning with T-ball at ages 7 and 8 and ending at Bigs for 18-year-olds. Each season is divided into league play and tournaments, which end with the Little League World Series played in Williamsport each August.

By the rules, the chairperson and coaches of every local program select among the 11- and 12-year-old players for an all-star team (or teams, depending on the size of the local program) to represent their community in the World Series tournament. Local programs compete with each other in single-loss elimination rules through districts and then play double elimination at the state and regional levels. The Little League World Series invites the winning teams from eight U.S. and eight international regions to compete for the championship cup in South Williamsport. Once teams arrive at the field complex, U.S. teams compete against each other and the international teams compete until one U.S. and one international team remain for the World Series championship.

Williamsport is a town of approximately 30,000. It was the "lumber capital of the world" in the 1880s and had the highest percentage of millionaires per capita in the United States at the turn of the 19th century. All that remains of those times is the nickname for the high school sports teams, the Millionaires. Today, nearly 15% of families live below the poverty line (23% of individuals). One quarter of youth (under 18) and one in 10 seniors are poor. With its annual budget of nearly $20 million, the Little League World Series headquarters is a valued business in the community. The 300,000 spectators who attend the Little League World Series bring additional millions in revenue to local business and taxes to local government. The town prepares for the 2-week event months in advance in order to ensure that teams, families, and fans enjoy the experience and the national media dwell on the positives of the event. Local hotels in a ten-mile radius are full for 2 weeks. Restaurants and local businesses do more business during the event than the rest of the year. Fifty local charities staff the food and souvenir booths at the Little League complex for the private vendor Delaware North Companies Sportservices and net a quarter of a million dollars each year.

In return for this business opportunity, the community staffs the activities and funds the extra services needed during the 2-week event. They manage traffic, increase medical support, and clean and decorate the streets. They provide an opening evening parade and picnic for the teams and parents; staff the Creighton J. Hale International Grove, where the teams, managers, and chaperones reside; and offer free parking and admission to fans. The community seems proud to host the event and to be known as the home of the Little League World Series. But a community online poll in the *Williamsport Sun Gazette* keeps the incentives clearly in focus.

What is the best part of the Little League World Series?

1. Collecting pins
2. Welcoming visitors
3. Realizing the financial boost
4. Watching the kids play
5. Getting to see celebrities

The Walt Disney Company owns ESPN, the television network that broadcasts every game of the U.S. regionals and the international World Series. ESPN is part of the American Broadcast Company and the Disney Channels (A&E, History, Biography, Military, Crime & Investigation, and Lifetime are sister channels). Disney broadcasts ESPN internationally (Europe, Asia, and Latin America) and ties the media together with publishing, music, films, websites, theme parks, and commercial merchandise—Disney stores, ESPN restaurants, Baby Einstein, the Muppets, and D.C. Comics. This is a partial list of Disney's holdings. Currently, ESPN/ABC pays $4.7 million each year to Little League for the rights to televise the games. That price means that the Little League World Series is treated like any other "show" on the ABC family of networks. It must be designed to sell enough advertising to turn a profit. In 2009, ESPN sold the titling rights and labeled its production the Little League World Series Presented by Kellogg's Frosted Flakes Reduced Sugar. And 15-year-old Moises Arias, from Disney's *Hannah Montana Show*, appeared as one of the color commentators during the games—not because he previously played Little League baseball, but because he was cast in a new Disney movie about the first international team that won the Little League World Series title.

ESPN/ABC uses 12 cameras to represent each game (they use the same number for major league games), and they send their leading baseball announcing teams to Williamsport. To elevate the narrative dynamics, they reduce the teams to featured players who "square off" against one another. These rivalries flare between different regions of the United States and culminate in the battle of nations in the final championship round. Interviews are held with winners, and cameras catch the preadolescents crying over a loss. Popular music is edited for the game promotions and transitions, and celebrities appear to endorse the League's intent and the games. Announcers continuously compare the kids with professional baseball players. Pitchers are little ___ (write in your favorite pitcher's name). Hitters are Albert Pujols. Infielders are Derek Jeter. And some World Series participants are labeled "five-tool players" (hit, throw, field, speed, and power) like Ken Griffey Jr. The effects of these comparisons are evident when the boys spit constantly; the pitchers cover their mouths with their mitts when talking to catchers or coaches; and the batters use two hands when adjusting their helmets, batting gloves, and jock straps between each pitch.

Reading the Little League World Series with sociological imagination reveals multiple layers of representation of boys playing baseball. At its root, Little League implies that boys are incapable of organizing themselves to play and require adult mediation of all elements of the game from international standards on rules of play, positions and playing time, and even uniform design. At its point of origin, Little League World Series is now a commodity; the town's single largest economic annual event, which Little League sells to Disney in order to fund its year-round operations. In turn, Disney through ESPN and ABC represent the Little League World Series as commercial spectacle while trying to persuade viewers that we are watching innocence and "pure sport." The boys are playing baseball; they are also playing for money, although not for personal benefit. Little League, Williamsport, and Disney reap the profits.

Without reading this text with sociological imagination, the ESPN/ABC representation of the Little League packages the experience for viewers in ways that substitute the image for the original; obscuring the processes of production of the text; and hiding the local human context, the history, and the decisions made across scale. The danger for me is that I lose contact with the people involved at all levels because a game among boys is re-presented as something that seems bigger and more important than everyday life. After all, Little League games are played nightly in 220,000 locations around the globe, and if I desire the experience of watching a game, I can just walk or ride to the local field. While there, I'll witness Little League practice of production without the mediation of spectacle. But if I'm really lucky and no Little League game is scheduled for that evening, I might find kids playing baseball who need a second baseman who has always had trouble hitting curveballs.

SHE LOVES YOU. YEAH, YEAH, YEAH

I might give the impression that I'm no damn fun at all because I take my efforts to read with sociological imagination from text to text, extracting any joy that might be there. "Geez, Pat, can't we just watch kids play baseball on TV and enjoy it?" Sure you can. The main danger for me is the role of institutions behind texts in mediating human contact through commercial transactions—the 11- and 12-year-old ball players are treated as commodities for sale to sponsors who are attempting to attract consumption from viewers of other commodities. As Guy Debord explained about the dangers of spectacles like the ESPN/ABC mediated Little League World Series Presented by Kellogg's Frosted Flakes Reduced Sugar, "All that was once directly lived has become mere representation" (1970, p. 1). The spectacle is an inverted image of society in which relations between commodities have supplanted relations between people, in which passive identification with the spectacle mediates human activity. At the moment that I am writing this chapter, there might be no better illustration of this phenomenon than the text *The Beatles: Rock Band*.

Full disclosure: I am a member of the Root Beer Beaver, a band that started in 1966 and re-formed with original members 8 years ago. Although spread around the United States now, the members assemble two or three times a year to practice and play for a local following in Fairport, New York. It's not unusual to see a couple hundred dancers on the floor at any one time with children jumping right next to their sliding, twisting, ponying, and jerking great-grandparents. Our repertoire begins with Arthur Big Boy Crudup's "That's All Right (Mama)" from 1946 and ends with the MC5's "Kick Out the Jams" from 1969 when the last of us graduated from high school. To be sure, this is a form of nostalgia, but the re-formation of the band and that music has helped members weather job loss, bankruptcy, business failure, children's accidents, and deaths of siblings and parents as we find new ways to support each other in something that approximates harmony. The people who come to hear us relive their youth perhaps, but they also share relationships with us, with each other, and with the music in ways that connect all of us directly and viscerally. I think this is what scared our parents originally. I'd like to report that the band is still loud, fast, and out of control, as rock and roll should be played, but all we promise now is that we are loud.

The Beatles: Rock Band is a video game that involves playing fake instruments in time with Beatles recordings. It's a variation of *Rock Band* (same concept with a variety of music simulated), which developed from a game called *Guitar Hero* (solo mimicry on a toy guitar). The various versions of such games are big business; music games are the second most popular video game, rivaling shooter/adventure series. According to the cofounder of Harmonix Music Systems (owned by MTV, a subsidiary of Viacom), playing such games requires an intense focus on the separate elements of a song because you must move your body in synchrony with the music in specific ways, and in turn, this forges a "deeper" connection with the music than just listening. In a simplified coding system of music notation, the screen directs the pretend John, Paul, George, and Ringo to move their fingers across the color-coded fret boards of the replica toy guitars and their arms and foot around a replica electronic drum kit. With whammy bars to "bend notes" and volume and tone controls, the simplified guitar models look like the ones the Beatles played during various stages of their careers, and the drums have "Ludwig" on the bass drum head right above the Beatles' unique logo. There are compatible versions for each of the three major video game systems. The price of the video and replica bass and drums is approximately $250, with an additional $100 for each replica guitar needed. Collarless Pierre Cardin suits are extra, I'm sure.

Behind the coding on the screen that directs the players' actions are video simulations of the Beatles playing the song as well. To obtain the Beatles' endorsement of the game, Harmonix had to appease the owners of the Beatles' legacy and Apple Corps—the surviving Beatles members, Paul McCartney and Ringo Starr, and the widows of John Lennon and George Harrison. For starters, Harmonix hired Giles Martin, the son of the Beatles' original music producer, who had worked with his father on several projects to re-release parts of the Beatles song list. The graphic designers for the game traveled to Apple Studio in London to experience the backdrops for records and viewed concert films in order to capture the dynamics of live performances. To render the likenesses of Beatles members accurately across time, costume designers and hair stylists were brought in to ensure that mop tops and outfits were precise. Despite these precautions, each of Apple Corps owners continued as consultants to ensure that the Beatles together and each member had been properly represented. According to the head of Harmonix, McCartney's advice was succinct: "Don't f__k this up."

McCartney and Starr endorse the game, although they both admit that they cannot play it well, or even properly, because the game coding is based on counting instead of feeling, and the recording arrests the song within a single version that will never change. In an interview with the *New York Times* (Radosh, 2009), McCartney said, "You want to get people engaged," and he sees the game as a logical extension of his teenaged pretending to be "Buddy Holly, Little Richard, Jerry Lee Lewis, and Elvis." Ringo is more circumspect about the game: "They're playing a game, they're not making music. The music is already made." Olivia Harrison, who backs the project, explained that her husband's response would have been, "Why don't they play real guitars?" Yoko Ono said, "It's like dancing." Even McCartney, who seemed most involved in the production, clarified his point by explaining that his pretending took place on stage while re-creating the original songs from those performers. Because other bands were "covering" the same songs on stage and stealing the thunder of the early Beatles, Lennon and McCartney started writing their own music for the Beatles to play.

Originally, the founders of Harmonix developed tools that would allow people without musical training to compose and play music. They discovered quickly, however, that people don't want to compose or play their own music; rather, they want to have a sense of what it's like to perform the songs they enjoy already. With Guitar Hero, they learned that buyers craved stage time as a "rock star" and not to participate in a musical experience. Rather than learn to be a musician or to be a participant in a musical event, the gamers wanted/want to have the experience earned by rock and rollers with "3 percent of the effort" and to appear before anyone watching as a rock star themselves. Betting that such desires are not limited to young men or women, Harmonix made the choice to produce a Beatles version of Rock Band as a calculated decision intended to expand its market to cover the spectrum of ages on the dance floor when the Root Beer Beaver plays in Fairport. McCartney considered it a wise business decision because the Beatles "are halfway between reality and mythology." Radosh ends his article with McCartney's musing about the future:

> In ten years' time you'll be standing there and you'll be Paul McCartney. You know that, don't you? You'll have a holographic case, and it will just encase you, and you'll be Paul McCartney. God knows what that will mean for me. . . . I'll be the guy on the original record.

Not wishing to trample on adult desires or fantasy role play, let me identify that the social relations mediated by *The Beatles: Rock Band* differ markedly from those the founders of Harmonix originally envisioned or those of the Root Beer Beaver and its dancers. Rather than being a musician (even one as crude as I am in the Beaver) or dancing to music recorded or live (ditto), users of the game substitute the choices of the producers and process of production in order to appear to be a member of the Beatles. The danger might be in the origins of the desire for this substitution and how it could be influenced, if not manufactured, commercially or even politically. McCartney sensed this difference as well when he remarked that he will remain Paul McCartney regardless of the technological texts that follow in order to further exploit rock star fantasies of the general public. He will be the one who produced music and social relationships around music and did not choose mimicking reproduction. Olivia Harrison assumes that George would have a similar doubt about why people would want to be John, Paul, George, or Ringo rather than "just play a guitar." And although the Beatles (and their widows) could be accused of repackaging themselves for profit one more time, they sense that there's something a little creepy about this game on their way to the bank.

TEXT EFFECTS

All text composers (regardless of medium or mode) design texts with intended meanings for an imagined, ideal reader. Perhaps the easiest example to imagine is advertisements in which an inscribed reader is thought to be a member of a target audience of consumers. Think fantastically elaborate texts about beer, trucks, and Viagra during televised football games or notice investment firm and insurance company themes and logos during PBS broadcasts of operas on Saturday afternoons. The composers picture their readers getting the message to desire and consume a commodity or idea. But composers of tweets, sexting, and Facebook pages imagine their "target" readers as well and make decisions accordingly. Differing media require special symbols and organizations in order to support the specificity of intended meanings, and perhaps that's why emoticons were invented—to add texture and clarity to email messages. Because all texts are targeted and tailored, they can be characterized as representing the sexuality, gender, age, class, race, or location of the composers and the ideal reader. The National Geographic Society was reacting to such characterizations when they advocated a ban on regular coordinate maps.

The effects of texts on readers regardless of medium are a matter of contention, however. Some argue a direct-effects theory of reading in which texts are capable of radically affecting people's beliefs and actions and, in effect, determining the meanings readers (viewers, listeners, and players) take away. Advocates of direct effects suggest a power imbalance in which composers direct readers' meaning and subsequent actions. This must be the story that advertising companies tell business and industry, and it's at least part of the rationale for struggles over text content of any medium and any context. The concerned assume the text will invite or cause certain desired or undesired ideas and actions, and advocate for or against the text. Consider calls to continue the Western literary canon in schools, to ban cigarette ads directed toward a youth market, to increase the specialized religious channels on cable television, to censor the children's book with gay penguins raising a chick, to boycott color segregation for infant and toddler clothing or to block President Obama's address to students from public schools. All adopt a direct effects theory for text reading. According to this model, text composers lead or push readers in fixed and predictable directions. Whether a direction is considered dangerous or not depends on the vantage point of the observer.

Others argue a theory that media texts simply reflect already established social forces, suggesting that both composers and readers are equally constrained. Composers can only create texts that conform basically to these forces or face the possibility of having their texts (intended messages) not being accepted or understood. Although texts might lead their readers in directions they are already headed, they cannot and do not lead them anywhere the composers desire because, if they venture too far beyond expectations, then their texts become incomprehensible or weird. Rather than a direct effect, advocates of this theory maintain that media texts simply reflect social tendencies. Advocates of a reflection theory argue that because we are a violent society we have violent media texts. Because our economy is based on consumption, our media texts project consumerism for us. We have biased maps because we have skewed worldviews. The literary canon is warranted because it reflects and reinforces the social forces that advanced Western society. In this explanation, readers seem to enjoy greater power over meaning than within a direct-effects model, holding composers of media texts loosely to acceptable forms and messages. Yet readers' meanings from texts are similarly fixed and predictable. They are set by social forces, however, and not invented by composers acting independently.

A third theory recognizes the possibility of directed influence through continuous exposure and the influence of social forces, but rejects the notion that meanings and effects of meanings can be predictable and fixed. It projects a potentially more active role for readers as they use text in order to continuously construct their personal and social identities. That is, readers can understand and use texts in ways that composers cannot predict or control. Across their teen years, Laura and Tim Pat reiterated this theory to me with every worry that I expressed about the texts in their lives. As a girl and teen, Laura explained that there is more than one way to use a Barbie or the Spice Girls or vampire literature. Tim Pat continues to explain that first-person shooter computer games and war literature can be the equivalent of his mother's puzzle-solving fetish in all media modes (*Lexulous* anyone?). Both argued that they use media texts of all types as background to their lives, and I shouldn't worry that the contentious texts that I identify will lead Laura to plastic surgery or Tim Pat to join Xe Services LLC.

Laura and Tim Pat take what they want from those and other texts in order to try on those identities to see what they like about them, and always in the nexus of all the texts that they have read in the past.

Although social forces produce what I understand to be sexist objects for females and violent militarism for males for economic and political gain, Laura and Tim Pat believe that they have agency to use these and any other texts for their own purposes. Laura used Barbie alteration narratives to invite talk among teenagers in a Young Women's Health Collective that she organized for her high school senior project and Tim Pat used the games to broker friendships at the school lunch table and uses the flows of information and the search for alternative solutions from the computer games in his work with critical GIS concerning incarceration in the United States. And come to think of it, I use the picture book *If You Give a Mouse a Cookie* to teach President Reagan's conservative attacks on social welfare programs during the 1980s. Laura Numeroff (1985) and Scholastic Books probably didn't have this use in mind when they published the book. My undergraduate and graduate students become wild eyed when they reconsider the relationship between that burdened little White boy and the insatiably needy rodent.

All these theories of the possible relationships between text (composers) and readers are possible and dangerous. And none is universal. That is, each explains the relationships in some contexts and not others. At times, drivers do stop at stop signs and they do drive at the posted speed limit. Yet in town, they know that a bump on the brakes is sufficient when no traffic is in sight. While on the highway in the middle of traffic flow, many realize that they have a 6- to 9-mile cushion above that limit (depending on the state, I'm told). These signs and driving itself become background to those who drive with cell phones in their hands, thumbs on the keyboards, or eyes on their GPS. Driving is not their priority during those moments and the signs are used as some comfort in the background that other drivers will act, at least somewhat, predictably. These examples demonstrate the contextual utility of the theories and also their physical dangers as well.

Together the theories imply that reading of text is a site of negotiation among composers, readers, and social forces within mundane and profound contexts (not all bumps on the brakes are equal, and minority drivers recognize the potential depths of the stop sign text). Like the cartographers, the composers of texts represent the world to and for readers, but readers have choices among the ways that they will read the map, and therefore represent themselves as readers and agents to their community and the world. Of course, the possibilities of choices assume that readers are practiced in flexible and different ways of reading.

IMAGINING PEDAGOGY

The first rule of teaching reading is to read aloud to whomever you're teaching. The act creates a text for listeners, demonstrating fluent reading, showing it's worth the effort, and enabling discussions of topics beyond the reading capacities of the audience. Part of the representation is the text chosen for the event, which to some degree provides a window to the reader's worldview. Each semester, I attempt to communicate these facts to the students in my classes, selecting texts carefully and making my choices of presentation public and explicit. I read aloud every class. Five weeks or so into a semester, I'll announce my intention to read *If You Give a Mouse a Cookie*. Among the undergraduate elementary education majors, invariably someone declares, "I love that book!"

The plot and the pen-and-ink-with-watercolor illustrations are simple and compelling. The book seems meant to be a cautionary tale— if you act, there will be consequences. A boy gives a mouse a cookie, and then the mouse wants a glass of milk, a napkin, a mirror, scissors for more grooming, a broom to clean up the mess he's made, a nap, a bedtime story, markers to extend the story's illustrations, tape to hang his masterpiece on the refrigerator, milk, and then another cookie. The mouse wears a backpack on the title page, suggesting that he and the boy are not intimates; and the boy's initial slight smile of friendship turns to puzzlement and resignation by the tale's end.

As always I ask for comments, and receive many, running from "It's cute" to "It reminds me of babysitting." When I state that the book was written in 1985 during the Reagan administration and that I think that it reflects his rhetoric about welfare in America, students look a bit confused and hurt. "It's a children's book?" "It's can't be about welfare!" The floodgates are open, however, and classmates become remarkably observant about the possibilities of that reading: "The poor are portrayed as vermin"; "Food, shelter, and jobs should be rights"; "The boy invites the mouse into his house and then resents that he is there. It's the story of U.S. slavery"; "The work for immigrants is menial"; "How could we have missed this"; and "Got any other of my favorites that you can ruin, Pat?" And, of course, I do.

This event is often a turning point for students' understanding of the processes of production of texts. We begin to discuss our decisions about how we design and construct read-aloud texts, how companies decide on which texts to publish and when, and how authors, even children's authors, choose to represent the world to readers. The last point is often a sticking point because many children's books do not seem morally didactic to them. In response, I quote Dr. Seuss, Maurice Sendak, and William Steig (interviewed by Jonathan Cott, 1983):

> I'm subversive as hell. . . . *The Cat in the Hat* is a revolt against authority. . . . It's revolutionary in that it goes as far as Kerensky, and then, stops. It doesn't go quite as far as Lenin. (p. 28)

> Adults will take their kids to museums to see a lot of peckers in a row on Roman statues and say, "That's art Dearie," and then, come home and burn *In the Night Kitchen.* Where's the logic in that? Art in people's minds is desexualized and that would make the great artists sick. (p. 55)

> When I wrote *Dominic*, I didn't mean it to be about anything. . . . I have a position, a point of view, but I don't have to think about it to express it. I write about anything and my view will come out. So when I am at work my conscious effort is to tell a story to readers. All this other stuff takes place automatically. (pp. 104–105)

READING THEORY

In the *Allegory of the Cave*, Plato warns readers that representations will always lead us away from the truth about social things because they block our access to their essence. Although I am not always consistent, I tend toward definitions of representation that assume social things do not have stable or inherent meanings (Hall, 1997). Rather through representation, people produce and circulate meanings according to their power within cultures and contexts. Think about poor Pluto or remember the Spring Creek Canyon mentioned in the introduction. There are no stable or true meanings for either.

Each representation mediates readers' meaning for Pluto, the Canyon, or any other text, supplying, competing, obstructing, fragmenting, and supplanting our understandings of the past, present, and future of these social things. In order to see how power circulates in representation, consider that the scientific order of cartographers thought it necessary to pass a formal resolution condemning the biases and use of the Mercator projection in school use. And yet that projection still adorns the walls of social studies classrooms and the pages of textbooks. Representation should be understood "as a relationship, as process, as the relay mechanism in exchanges of power, value, and publicity" (Mitchell, 1995, p. 420).

As an undergraduate, I read Guy Debord's *The Society of the Spectacle* (1970) and Herbert Marcuse's *One-Dimensional Man* (1964), which argued that media representations were the contemporary means of social control, inveigling citizens to passivity through spectacular images of consumption. Debord labeled this process of representation "a permanent opium war" of pacification, and Marcuse called it "repressive tolerance," commodifying rebellion and selling it back to youth. Both concluded that media representations seek to separate citizens from one another and from producing their lives through individual and collective actions, leaving them eager to produce and consume commodities and to seek more opulent spectacles. Their concerns seem relevant today. For example in Disney's hands, preteen boys playing baseball is made to seem impossible without a corporate sponsor, celebrities, and hoopla.

For Jean Baudrillard (1988), the time of spectacle passed when citizens became more interested in image (and images) than they did in commodity production or consumption. That is, commodities are produced, distributed, and consumed for their projected social meanings and exchange values, separate from their use value. We consume the power, prestige, and status socially and emotionally produced around manufactured things. The image of a sports car conveys virility. The representation surrounding the iPad connotes 21st-century hipness and extensive social network(ing) connections beyond the norm. *CSI Miami* bathes watchers in sun, sex, and danger of their imagined social lives. We construct our identities from these images (regardless of our realities) in order to "picture yourself on a boat on a river . . ." as one of the lads in *Beatles: Rock Band*.

Reading for social competence only makes us vulnerable to representation of spectacle or "hyperreality," as Baudrillard called it. It undercuts our agency, influencing our decisions involved in our production of our lives. To varying degrees, each theorist called for a type of reading with sociological imagination in order to resist, if not tame, the power of media representation. Baudrillard thought that citizens should take up media representations at face value and ruin the economy by obeying the commands to continuously consume in order to achieve their ever changing images of themselves. Perhaps the worldwide Great Recession of 2008 was the beginning of Baudrillard's solution. Debord called for detournement in which the liberation of everyday life could be sought through uses of media representation against itself in order to divert, distract, and redirect readers' gaze. Today groups such as Adbusters Media Foundation and Guerilla Girls seem to practice detournement to considerable effect. In *Reading the Popular* (1989), John Fiske presents the strongest case for reader agency, liberating readers from the possibility of oppression because they use media representation for their own purposes rather than comply with the ascribed meanings. While my kids taught me that Fiske could be correct at times, my daily life tells me this might be a romanticized view of agency.

CHAPTER 3

Do I Control
the Meaning of Texts?

I seem to be in charge of meaning while I'm reading. I bring my past experiences, my knowledge, and my purposes to bear on the text, using them as I see fit or so it seems, until I acknowledge that I am using social processes to accomplish social goals while I'm reading. My experiences and knowledge are social as well—even my most private thoughts are formed in socially constructed language. Perhaps our independence is overstated because the social is deeply embedded in the personal, extending and limiting our reading according to social practices and social frames that others established often outside our classroom doors. The tradition of closing our classroom doors (or the gates behind us) can't separate the social from the personal.

Did you receive your bonus yet? I've been waiting for mine since the Bush administration asked Congress for $700 billion dollars during the fall of 2008 in order to prevent the collapse of the American economy. President Bush and his BOGSAT considered some financial institutions *too big to fail* and sought government intervention. After a short public fuss, they acknowledged that bonus incentives were necessary to keep *indispensable* Wall Street employees in place to lead us toward an eventual recovery. I've been checking my mailboxes at home and at work daily, but I have yet to be notified that I am indispensable or that my institution is too big to fail. I'm sure it's an oversight.

Administration officials chose their words carefully when making their request to Congress. Let's face it. Their request seemed to be a contradiction of their previous 8-year stance in favor of free markets and against government regulation or involvement. Yet just before they were to leave office, administration officials secured the equivalent of the annual U.S. military budget in order to prop up some of the teetering Wall Street institutions. Delivered with alarm and trembling voices, the administration's frame, too big to fail, evoked images of heroism, not contradiction. They were saving the nation, if not the world.

Consider how the words worked: too, big, to fail. In the United States, size matters. Bigger is better. Big houses, big stores, big television screens, and big cell phone networks are all associated with wealth, status, and progress. Failure is out—unacceptable. The United States must succeed. It is our destiny. Big and successful are important parts of the American dream. The administration's words, then, set parameters for subsequent thinking and talk, inviting some ideas and blocking others. *Too big to fail* connotes impending danger and positions all American readers to accept the administration's proposed solution. Who wants to be seen as opposing the American dream? That's the purpose of framing an issue, an argument, or an event—using words, symbols, and images to position readers' thinking, discussion, and action.

MY BONUS

Within government's funding for institutions too big to fail and bonuses for employees considered vital to the economic recovery, I should be a shoo-in. Although Bush's proposal did not mention education explicitly, Bush had argued previously that education is vital to American economic prosperity. In fact, the Bush 1, Clinton, Bush 2, and Obama administrations all framed education as the institution responsible for the development of human capital—the individual and collective knowledge and skills that will make the American economy competitive, if not predominant, in a global economy. In a postindustrial society, we're told, knowledge and those skills are all that citizens have to sell in order to make a living, and these skills are the assets that their employers buy in order to continue to innovate in goods and services and create wealth. Within this conception of the relationship between education and the economy, I'm well positioned in the supply chain of highly qualified teachers who have, do, and will staff the public education system in the United States, reviving and maintaining the new economy.

Although it might be immodest for me to say so, I am responsible for producing human, social, or cultural capital within my students that they can sell eventually in order to become elementary school teachers. Here's how the numbers work, because my case for a bonus is evidence-based. The 50 knowledgeable and able college students whom I teach

each year graduate, pass certification exams, become employed, and then contribute to the knowledge and skills of 20 to 25 students each year. That makes me highly productive, and responsible for 1,000 to 1,250 "highly capitalized dividends" annually. I've been doing this consistently for 30 years, which makes me personally responsible for 30,000 to 38,000 knowledgeable and able workers in the American economy.

According to the logic of human capital development theory, everything else should fall neatly into place. My students will teach their students how to pass proficiency exams, leading to more schooling, test passing, and eventually to gainful employment within the knowledge economy. As the economy shifts, these tested employees will be able to recapitalize themselves in order to keep several steps ahead of the educated citizens from other countries. Through this supply system, the United States should continue to lead the global economy, enabling all citizens to enjoy middle-class or higher lifestyles. By the federal government's logic then, it's pretty clear that my institution is vital to the economy, and I am indispensable!

Despite my reasoned, personal reading of the federal proposal to save the economy, my bonus check has neither been cut nor delivered. Although I can invoke the too-big-to-fail frame—if teacher education fails, the American economy and dream suffer—my reading of the too-big-to-fail text is not in my control. Despite being 100% successful for 30 years on the development of human, social, and cultural capital, I'm passed over and bonuses are paid instead to bankers and brokers who submerged the world's financial system, leading to the Great Recession, credit defaults, and higher unemployment. These acts seem counterintuitive, until I connect the too-big-to-fail frame and the education-as-human-capital-development frame with an appropriate set of underlying values.

Although I could make a personally persuasive case for my bonus, I failed to recognize that values behind the administration's economic and educational frames made my reading of the too-big-to-fail text seem odd at best. The too-big-to-fail and education-as-human-capital-development frames stem from the same set of values that has distinguished the discourse of federal administrations' BOGSAT for the past 30 years. Michel Foucault (1970) used the term *discourse* to signify a unifying set of values for a group. Within any society, multiple discourses exist (expressing differing political, economic, cultural, social, religious, regional, and other sets of values), and they compete with one another in order to be considered relevant, if not controlling, in every situation. The frame *too big to fail* was a tool and a weapon within that competition, working to rally group members and the undecided to its cause and to batter competing frames and discourses into silence. Although the stakes aren't always as high as saving the American economy, the competitions to have particular sets of values define the situation are always present in all situations. Framing, then, is an attempt to gain power in the discussion of issues, arguments, or events, setting boundaries on what will be considered appropriate thoughts and actions and what will be judged to be inappropriate, abnormal, and even subversive.

The discourse behind these two frames values market competition as the engine for all social change. Accordingly, unless there is competition among alternatives vying for the affections of the public on every matter, stagnation will follow, because without competition, those involved will have little incentive to alter previous ways of working, thinking, or being. Markets put alternatives to the test of consequences, letting consumers pick among them, shifting resources in the direction of particular alternatives and neglecting others. Once stronger alternatives are proved and readily available, the weaker ones are abandoned. Joseph Schumpeter (1962) called this process *creative destruction*. Although continuously creative by bringing the "new" and "better" alternatives to consumers, market competition destroys previously viable and new, but weaker, alternatives. When markets are the primary value, everything is temporary, because a better-than-current alternative will eventually emerge. Within this discourse, the market—that is, the consumer— decides the future, and the role for government and all other institutions is to support market competition in every way possible.

To this way of thinking, government funding to financial institutions was simply a logical act, overcoming the "unforeseen" effects of previously effective financial alternatives. Given brief support, the financial market will right itself soon, because market entrepreneurs will invent new more effective alternatives. To stimulate innovation, then, bonuses were required to keep the creative people in place. Without those bonuses, talent would gravitate to competing parts of the economy, which offered preferable incentives for them to employ their knowledge and skill sets. The discourse justifies the frame—at least within its logic.

My reading and creative use of the frames fails in securing my bonus, because I did not consider their underlying discourse of market competition. I did not propose innovative markets to supply teachers ready to push human capital development to its peak. Although I thought that I understood their frames to my advantage, I actually violated the values of the market discourse behind the frames, because I relied on government regulations and not the free market to make my case. That is, state governments control access to teacher certification and require wannabe teachers to graduate from a teacher education program in order to be considered highly qualified. Although a few alternative routes exist to become a teacher, university and college teacher education programs don't compete fundamentally with each other. According to the market discourse, teacher education programs are not too big to fail, and I am not indispensable to the economic recovery.

In general, frames attempt to direct my reading of social things, setting parameters around how I should think, speak, and act. The discourses behind frames influence which readings will seem acceptable and which will seem odd to the general public. In my example, my personal alignment of the government's frames was undercut by a market discourse, positioning my reading as self-serving, even counterproductive to the possibilities of market-driven teacher education. Yet my evidence-based argument stands—those 38,000 citizens contribute to American society daily. In order to investigate, perhaps even interrogate, frames and the discourses behind them, readers will have to use their sociological imaginations to look carefully at how the terms and symbols work in texts in order to determine the dangers in the positions they offer. Damn, I wanted that bonus.

FRAMES FOR EDUCATION

The free market discourse has made its way into public education as well, despite the original framing of public schooling as the mechanism for liberal democracy. Thomas Jefferson (1816) wrote, "If a nation expects to be ignorant and free, in a state of civilization, it expects what never was or never will be." Schools would enlighten citizens, who would use that knowledge to form a government that would ensure their freedom and well-being. To be sure, there were limits to Jefferson's vision for schooling and democracy. Only sons of White landowners would work their way past basic schooling in order to lead a meritocratic United States. Women, minorities, and the poor were to be excluded from secondary and postsecondary levels of schooling, and they remained so well into the 20th century. Excluded groups' efforts to gain the rights of full participation are etched in the federal educational policy over time. For example, the Elementary and Secondary Education Act (ESEA) was amended to include the poor (Title I, 1965), disabled (Title VI, 1966), bilingual (Title VII, 1967), and women (Title IX, 1972). When commissioner of education Francis Keppel (1965) signed the original act, he stated:

> Archimedes told us many centuries ago: "Give me a lever long enough and a fulcrum strong enough and I can move the world." Today, at last, we have a prospect of a lever long enough and supported strongly enough to do something for our children of poverty. The lever is education, and the fulcrum is federal assistance.

Contrast Keppel's extension of Jefferson's words with the framing of education within the report *A Nation at Risk* (National Commission on Excellence in Education, 1983), published during President Reagan's first term. In the latter work, public schools became the United States' problem, and the official goal of schooling shifted from strengthening an inclusive democracy to maintaining economic and political leadership in the world. These changes were captured in the opening lines.

> The educational foundations of our society are presently being eroded by a rising tide of mediocrity that threatens our very future as a Nation and a people. . . . If an unfriendly foreign power had attempted to impose on America the mediocre educational performance that exists today, we might well have viewed it as an act of war. (p. 3)

Think about the words of this frame and the associations they invite. Let's be clear, that rising tide of mediocrity referred to the students mentioned in the titles of ESEA. They are eroding America's future. School personnel who work with them are traitors, aiding America's economic and political enemies. At the same time, these words position critics of public schools as patriots, fighting bravely against foreign powers. According to the BOGSAT behind *A Nation at Risk*, America was (is) losing its competitive edge, not because of poor business or government decisions, but because of the consequences of 1960s discourses of inclusion, which forced schools to treat citizens more equitably.

After 30 years of government officials, businesspeople, and philanthropists repeating this message through multiple media outlets, commonsense thinking "requires" dramatic school reform according to market principles or the United States will slip to third world status. In almost every way imaginable, however, this frame is wrong. Let me start with international comparison. Despite continuous government and media cheerleading to the contrary, American institutions are not number 1; and it has little directly to do with public schooling. Consider democracy, prosperity, and freedom of the press.

> According to the conservative British news weekly the *Economist*, the United States was 18th on its annual Democracy Index (2008), slightly below the mean among the 30 full democracies, and well above the cutoff to be classified as flawed. Among the full democracies, however, the U.S. scored at or near the bottom on electoral process, civil liberties, and functioning of government.

> The philanthropic branch of Dubai's Legatum Group ranked the United States 9th in prosperity among the 104 nations (2009). While we were considered first in entrepreneurship and innovation, the United States was listed 27th in health care. Education was ranked 7th, higher than economic fundamentals, safety, governance, personal freedom, and social capital.

> In 2009, Freedom House listed the United States as tied with Czech Republic and Lithuania for 24th place in freedom of the press. The report cited concerns for the United States' wavering legal environment concerning the protection of news sources, increasing political pressures to shield government information from public view, and declining economic support for independent news outlets.

Eighteenth in democracy, 9th in prosperity, and 24th in free press point toward problems in American society that have little to do with inclusion of the poor, minorities, and women in schools, although those issues could be taken seriously within school curricula. What does it mean that, among full democracies, the United States had the lowest score concerning civil liberties, that U.S. social capital was rated lowest among the top ten most prosperous countries, or that U.S. commitment to the First Amendment to its Constitution is ranked in the middle of the pack of "free presses"? Outside the *Nation at Risk* frame and the market discourse behind it, these comparisons provide a different agenda for anyone interested in the United States' slippage among the world's nations. Moreover, those rankings suggest flaws in the rationales for reforming public schools, and they imply that schools are not the taproot of America's problems.

FOLLOW THE SCORES

Originally, the *Nation at Risk* BOGSAT argued that academic standards were becoming so low that children were unlikely to reach the education status of their parents and grandparents. The basic data behind this claim were spelling errors in some job applications, surveys that identified that adolescents were more familiar with popular culture than with historical dates and dead presidents, and . . . well, nostalgia. In 1990, secretary of energy James Watkins commissioned Sandia Laboratories to document the decline. The subsequent report, however, could not substantiate the claims of decline, demonstrating instead increasing scores for each demographic subgroup that took the SAT test. I won't claim to understand how aggregate test scores can decline while the subgroup scores increase, but I know the name of the theory behind how it's possible—*Simpson's paradox* (and I don't mean Homer). In Watergate-like intrigue, government officials never released the *Sandia Report on U.S. Achievement Scores* to the public, and in 1993, Projected Censored called this act "a perfect lesson in censorship." On average, today's students are smarter than those who attended school during previous decades.

The international comparisons are even more complex. First, American students' scores are always well above the mean of countries in all comparisons. For the 2007 Trends in International Mathematics and Science Study (TIMSS), American 4th-graders placed 9th in math and 5th in science among 36 countries and 8th-graders were 6th in math and 9th in science among 48 countries. In 2006, American 4th-grade students were statistically tied with 12 countries for 3rd on the Progress in International Reading Literacy (PIRLS) test. Compared with U.S. rankings on democracy, prosperity, and freedom of the press, American achievement scores are much higher!

Yet when educational psychologist David Berliner (2006) disaggregated the American scores by race and social class, he found that the United States has two public school systems—one for Whites and the middle class and another for students of color and the poor. On the TIMSS and the PIRLS, American scores showed a perfect negative correlation between poverty and achievement in math, science, and reading. American students from schools with the least poverty were the top scorers internationally, and those from schools with over 75% of the students receiving free or reduced lunch subsidies fell well below the international average. Berliner connected these findings to race in two ways. First, he demonstrated that the minority students were more likely to be enrolled in poverty schools, and second, he showed that the United States had the greatest difference in average test scores between suburban and urban schools, citing resegregation of housing in the country.

Berliner's work challenges the exclusionary discourses that argue that poor and minority students on average are not smart enough or disciplined enough to perform at levels comparable with their financially better off and White counterparts. For example, in *The Bell Curve*, Richard Herrnstein and Charles Murray (1994) concluded, "For many people, there is nothing they can learn that will repay the cost of the teaching" (p. 520). Let me unpack this sentence, because it is one of the most pessimistic remarks about education and human capacity that I have ever encountered. The first clause—*for many people*—connotes that a large group of Americans is being considered. *There is nothing they can learn* suggests to any good English speaker that they are referring to the absence of abilities (not opportunity). And finally, *will repay the cost of teaching* declares that our associations with one another should be ruled by cost efficiencies. Money is all that binds us together.

Although President Obama acknowledges that he benefited from affirmative action social support programs originating in the 1960s, he echoes the second assumption about undisciplined cultures around poverty and race. When he retells the story of his mother waking him at 4 o'clock in the morning to do his homework, he invokes ant and grasshopper narratives that assume that some cultures are pathological and poorly adaptive to the changing environments of our living. What members of these cultures need, he argues, is a heavy dose of middle-class, Protestant qualities applied directly in order to make something out of themselves. Just roll up the sleeves of those poor and minority preschoolers and get their adolescent siblings out of bed at 4:00, and schools will take care of the achievement score gap quickly.

Berliner does not deny cognitive or cultural difference among individuals and groups, but he accepts neither of Herrnstein and Murray's

nor President Obama's frames for reading the separate-and-unequal results of schooling. Berliner confronts the claim that intelligence is hereditary, fixed, and raced. Genetics is not my field, but our daughter,
Laura, is an expert. "Dad," she says with the tired tone of a daughter
who is much smarter than her father, "Lewontin demonstrated that two
genetically identical seeds of corn planted in very different plots would
grow to different heights. In good soil, water, and sun, genes account for
almost all of the noticeable variation in the plants. But in bad soil, without adequate water or sun, genes cannot express themselves, and they
account for little variation among the lower growing and sickly plants."
Even I can fill in this blank. If the genes can't express themselves, the
environment accounts for most of the variation. Laura explained this
metaphor as if she couldn't understand how educators could miss this
relationship, that is, unless they let exclusionary discourses direct their
uses of scientific evidence.

In his book *Intelligence and How to Get It: Why Schools and Culture
Count*, psychologist Richard Nisbett (2009) argues that human genes respond to the quality of the human environment. At the top of the socioeconomic status scale, nearly 75% of the variation in intelligence results
from genetic influences, but in poverty, less than 20% of the variation
in intelligence is caused by genetic endowment. Poor people's environments account for 80% of the variation because inadequate environments suppress gene expression. Although these findings have many
implications, they show clearly that Herrnstein and Murray are wrong—
intelligence is not primarily hereditary or fixed; rather, genetic contribu-
tions vary according to richness of the environment in an almost perfect
correlation. Adequate food, housing, health care, and income and relief
of the anxiety surrounding struggles to obtain those qualities of life are
the metaphors of good soil for corn. And the United States is not headed
in a good direction on these matters. The Brookings Institute's Metropol-
itan Policy Program reported that 30% of Americans (91 million people)
are below or hover just above the official poverty line (Kneebone & Garr,
2010) and the Children's Defense Fund (2010) chronicles that number
includes 40% of the nation's children. Berliner (2006) calls for teachers
to join others working for adequate housing, health care, food, and income security for those Americans who need it, and he points toward the
countries above America on all the democracy, prosperity, and free press
indexes as evidence that such programs work. Many of their achievement scores are high as well.

Advocates of the human capital frame and underlying market discourse argue that the federal educational law No Child Left Behind (NCLB) acknowledged the dual education system when it required schools to disaggregate test scores on state exams. Accordingly, schools reported test scores separated by class, race, English language proficiency, and ability in order to demonstrate that all groups took the tests and made adequate yearly progress. These tests covered achievement in reading, mathematics, and science and were administered annually from 3rd to 8th grades and then once in high school. All students were required to be proficient by 2014. If a school failed to make annual progress, it was subject to punitive sanctions, reducing funding and eventually closing the school, if progress was not forthcoming. Progress was monitored in two ways. State tests measured progress toward state standards, and the National Assessment of Educational Progress measured progress toward national norms.

Whether or not NCLB worked depends on to whom one listens. The Bush 2 administration claimed progress annually, but shared little data with the public. The think tank Education Trust published a report in 2006 that argued Americans had reasons to be optimistic about NCLB progress. Elementary schools made modest gains in helping students to become proficient in reading and math, middle schools had inched forward, and secondary schools remained constant. Although the report acknowledged that test scores in some schools and states had actually declined during the NCLB, on average the report concluded that the law was working, albeit slowly. To accelerate its impact, Education Trust (Hall & Kennedy, 2006) recommended that middle and high school teachers mimic their elementary counterparts and focus their attention more directly on the tested information through standardized and commercially marketed curricula.

The Civil Rights Project (CRP) at the University of California, Los Angeles (Lee, 2006), however, argued that NCLB progress was an illusion. Looking at the same statistics as the Bush administration and Education Trust, the CRP found neither a significant rise in achievement scores nor the closure of the racial gap. At the current rate of growth, they maintained, only 34% of American students would be proficient by 2014 according to the NAEP data (not the 100% goal), and only 24% of poor and minority students would make it past the proficiency threshold. These projections are in sharp contrast to the claims of state governments based on their state tests. For example, Alabama reported 83%

proficiency among readers according to their state exam, but NAEP recorded only 22% proficiency among Alabama students. New Jersey published that 82% were proficient on state tests, but NAEP found only 37%. Oregon's numbers were similar—81% according to the state and 29% on the NAEP. There were achievement discrepancies between state and federal tests in every state, although some gaps were smaller than others.

These discrepancies strike me as similar to the Dow Jones Index during the fall of 2008. At the fall equinox, Wall Street claimed 14,000 points represented American capital accumulation and economic power, but by winter solstice, less than 8,000 points remained. Pundits said that the Dow (and the country) lost the 6,000 points. However, if we "lost" those points (that wealth), where did they go? And who found them? Do you see what I mean? Only real things like keys, homework, and pounds can be lost. If those Dow numbers were real or even if they were like the human, social, and cultural capital that I helped to create, then we'd be able to trace the wealth somewhere. But Wall Street built virtual capital that was never real, and therefore, it couldn't be lost. Those 6,000 points and all they represent just disappeared. America and Americans were never as rich as the newspapers, radio, television, and Internet reported blindly, as if the Dow Index were as important as Yankee scores to all Americans. The Wall Street bankers who made those points appear, but then disappear, created a virtual rise and then a real collapse.

Virtual capital is a metaphor for state educational achievement discrepancies. In the light of the NAEP, state scores represented virtual achievement because the achievement never actually existed. Rather, it was cooked like the Wall Street banks' books, with state education departments adopting lower standards and easier tests in order to exceed NCLB mandates. The CRP connected virtual achievement directly to the two educational systems within American public schools. The state scores "underestimate the racial and socioeconomic achievement gaps" (Lee, 2006, p. 6). While states were twice as likely to inflate White students' achievement levels, they were four times more likely to overstate Black and poor student proficiency in reading and math. Just as the drop in the Dow hit hardest against poor and minority citizens, virtual achievement punishes them more as well.

My reading of these test scores with sociological imagination suggests that it's dangerous for the federal government to trade standardization of education policy for attention to the issues of poverty. In an analogy with the traffic signs on my trip home from Grinnell College, the apparent standardization of schools' responsibilities through testing masks the unequal social life of public schooling. When examined outside the current iterations of the parameters of *A Nation at Risk* frame, school curricula and instruction do not appear to be able to overcome the effects of poverty sufficiently to close the achievement gaps between a significant number of the 40% of children living at or near the poverty line and the 60% who are more secure concerning food, shelter, income, health care, and safety. The test score evidence suggests that the federal official frame discourages the very types of thinking necessary to address the realities of making public schools a place where a more inclusive version of Jefferson's original frame for public schooling could be realized.

READING THE DISCOURSE, NOT JUST THE FRAME

Although the Brookings Institute's report on poverty identified a wavering sense of security among that 60% of American children, federal officials are reluctant to move off the market discourses in order to address poverty and its effects on schooling. As Berliner (2006) explained, after the Great Society's War on Poverty of the 1960s, in which programs for housing, income, health care, and schooling were coordinated, the achievement test score gaps between minority and majority and poor and middle-class students began to close. Ignoring this evidence of the benefits of enriched soil, the Obama administration offered a new name for the same frame for public school reform policies. Recognizing that students could change their achievement proficiency status simply by stepping over a state border to a different set of standards, the Obama administration earmarked Great Recession stimulus funding in order to entice state governors to commit to national common core education standards for reading and mathematics.

In many ways, this was a remarkable feat. Common core standards smack of a national curriculum—a proposal that drew loud protests from states during the 1960s when the ESEA was written, and again in the 1980s, when the first President Bush attempted America 2000 goals. With their state budgets in tatters from the Great Recession, however, 48 governors charged the National Governors Association and Council of Chief State School Officers to assemble a BOGSAT in order to hammer out an overall set of internationally comparative high school graduation goals. Once those goals were articulated in 2009, national K–12 curricula standards were written to ensure that all graduates would be ready for a career or college—the new goal for American schools. With the guidance of ACHIEVE, the nonprofit educational reform arm of the national Business Roundtable, the common core standards were developed. In 2010, the federal government awarded a $350 million bid to the Partnership for Assessment of Readiness for College and Career (PARCC) to develop national assessment systems to monitor K–12 progress toward those goals. The Pearson publishing company has the rights to market PARCC products to the nation's schools.

To induce states to adopt these standards, the Obama administration set aside $4.5 billion as part of his Race to the Top school reform agenda. States would compete for federal contracts to reform their schools. Although the administration stated that it was for alternative routes to reform, three criteria had to be included within the proposal. First, states would adopt the common core standards and assessment systems to follow. Second, they would tie teacher evaluation to student test scores directly in a value-added system (compare students' scores yearly). Finally, they would permit competitive alternative routes to teacher certification and encourage more charter schools (that would work outside school district and state regulations). Over 30 states submitted proposals, often with $250,000 grants from the Bill and Melinda Gates Foundation, and two were picked during the first round, winning hundreds of millions of dollars to fund their reform. All schools were invited to resubmit for a second round after they rewrote their proposals to align more directly with the stated criteria. Eight were successful in the second round. The remaining states were thanked for their participation.

Obama's Race to the Top frame feeds on the market discourse explicitly. *Race* tells us that education is a competition and, by inference, that we are competing with all others near and far. *The top* is where Americans want to be. Perhaps the sports metaphor is too obvious for Obama and his basketball-playing secretary of education, but the stakes for communities and citizens seem much greater than a simple win-loss record. Races have winners, and losers; and the top has limited space. If states, school districts, schools, and teachers must compete with each other in order to continuously innovate, then what does that mean for students, particularly those whose environments have been allowed to decline to a point where basic needs are not secured and expressions of their genetic potentials are in doubt. Within the frame and the discourse behind it, it's assumed that the market will provide. But clearly, it has not for tens of millions of Americans to this point.

Frames, and discourses behind them, influence our reading of social texts, expanding and limiting the meanings we make. Through the terms and symbols that represent the frames, designers seek to set parameters for our thinking, talking, and acting, seeking to position us. We are therefore not in personal control of the meanings we make—able to do whatever we wish with text. I didn't get a bonus. Recognizing how frames work in the struggle of discourses for power over interpretation can help readers to employ their sociological imagination in efforts to choose to accept or resist the dangers inherent in the positions offered them within a certain time and place. And we might well decide to read the same frame with social competence in some contexts and then with sociological imagination in others. When we do choose to resist popular frames because we have become aware of how they endanger us in ways we find unacceptable, some people will likely see our reading as inappropriate, odd, impractical, counterproductive, cynical, subversive, and even destructive personally and socially. At those times, we must remember that our readings and our ethico-political choices connect us personally with the social. Others have made similar readings of those social texts and similar choices about the main dangers. We can act personally or find others to act with us to confront the dangers behind those texts.

IMAGINING PEDAGOGY

The Dynamic Indicators of Basic Early Literacy (DIBELS) test is framed as a scientifically based tool for screening early readers on their speed and accuracy in letter names, initial sounds, phonemic segmentation, nonsense words, oral reading, and retelling. Often, parents mention their child's DIBELS classification when enrolling them in summer reading camp. As preparation for working with these children, our master's students studying to be reading specialists investigate the frame and discourses behind the DIBELS test. Virtually all our students know the DIBELS brand from their work in schools; they understand it was developed in accordance with the National Reading Panel Report; and they realize that the officials of the federal government "recommended" its use within the Reading First Initiative of NCLB. Yet many are ambivalent about the power of DIBELS to position young readers as "intensive," "strategic," or "regular" and teachers as responsible to provide curricular cures for identified deficits.

From looking at the DIBELS website (www.dibels.org), the master's students recognize the discourse of experimental science. The producers of DIBELS use scientific language, logic, and appearance in order to claim the test's legitimacy in schools. Because its production followed the standards set in the National Reading Panel Report and the Education Science Reform Act of 2002, school personnel can rely on the authority of DIBELS. Those who might question its value or power are positioned as unscientific. On the same site, however, it becomes clear that business practices and values mediate the claims of objectivity of science. DIBELS is an educational commodity as well as a scientific tool, and as a commodity, it must compete with other screening tests on the reading assessment market that was created when scientists determined that early monitoring of students' reading development could prevent later reading disabilities. Although the basic materials of DIBELS can be downloaded for free and can be scored for $1 per student, the basic materials, support materials, and technological and human support are available commercially in several forms for those states and school districts that desire help with its implementation and consequences.

On the website, it's clear also that the federal government had a direct hand in creating the market for DIBELS through the Reading First Initiative of the NCLB. Relying on the discourses of science and business, federal and state officials established the conditions for DIBELS production, purchase, and use. In addition, the policies created an official protocol for reporting progress through DIBELS scores. Googling away from the DIBELS and Reading First websites, master's students find that the Department of Education inspector general identified a conflict of interest among several government officials appointed to oversee the implementation of Reading First policies across the country, who recommended DIBELS to states departments of education and school districts, and then profited from those sales.

Examining the frame and discourses of DIBELS deepened master's students' understandings of its power within their schools and over the lives of young readers. While DIBELS producers claim science as the rationale for its objective legitimacy in schools, the master's students learned that subjective commercial principles and practices mediated the science and that partisan government involvement mediated the free market. Contrary to free market rhetoric, the distortions in market resulted from a lack of government regulation rather than from too much regulation. Reading DIBELS's frame and discourses with socio-logical imagination, they learn how the meanings of DIBELS are remark-ably complex, contextual, and social and that its power is historically contingent and not a natural outcome of its science. And within those meanings, they can find their agency to resist the positions that DIBELS offers young children and them.

READING THEORY

My somewhat systematic thoughts about the social influences on mean-ing and the relationships between agency and social structures began with this quote:

> Men make their own history, but they do not make it just as they please; they do not make it under circumstances chosen by themselves but under circumstances directly found, given and transmitted from the past. (Marx, 1969, p. 15)

To me, the quote engenders hope. If people make history, then they can remake those parts that they deemed objectionable. When I first read the passage during the middle of the Vietnam War, the War on Poverty, and the civil rights movement and at the beginning of feminist revolu-tion, there seemed to me to be a lot of new history to make. Yet problems endured because they were "found, given and transmitted" in ways that curbed, if not stymied, my (our) effort to make a different history. We couldn't think, talk, and act our ways toward change, because decisions made in the past framed our lives in physical and ideological structures regardless of whether changes were in our best material interests. Rather, like my ride back from Grinnell College, the social texts of my life at the time invited me to embrace the social competence of a consumer of goods and services, expert opinion, idealized representations of the past, and spectacle of celebrity and success. In order to make new history, I had to confront that historical positioning.

At the time, my brothers and sisters in flannel were certain that Thomas Hobbes and the other English philosophers were wrong—we had not consciously entered a political arrangement with the state in or-der to avoid chaos. We were pretty sure that we wanted chaos. And it seemed at the time that there were too many of us in the United States and around the Western world to accept the notions of Montesquieu and other French Enlightenment philosophers that citizens were socialized into the status quo, and we were simply slow learners. In 1968, when the French Communist Party betrayed the general strike for a more inclusive government and Richard Nixon beat Hubert Humphrey in the U.S. presidential election, however, it became clear that majorities in Western societies chose the history that was found and given and transmitted to the one in the making. How was it possible that so many people would primarily read for social competence and chose change as the main danger?

In his *Outline of a Theory of Practice*, Pierre Bourdieu (1977) argued that social structures do not force individuals toward acceptance of the status quo; rather, the structures create environments (frames) that invite and compel individuals to choose to fit in. In this way, he develops a middle ground between Hobbes's conscious choice and Montesquieu's version of social conditioning. Social competence is simultaneously a result of the found, given, and transmitted and an individual's typically unconscious choosing to belong and to get along. Bourdieu labels these environments as "habitus, systems of durable, transportable dispositions," which regulate without obvious regulation or regulator. At the same time, individuals choose to act in predictable, if somewhat idiosyncratic, ways. In this way, the structures work on the individual, while over time, individuals can work to affirm or subtly subvert the structures. In this light, agency does not guarantee change within social structures, but offers its possibility.

Held in place by the relative power of competing discourses, the framing of text commands our attention, offers us positions of competence, and rewards specific meanings as normal. Frames can only invite us to fit in general; they cannot secure our acquiescence within particular contexts. While framing positions us, it cannot determine how we will read the frame with unique arrays of discourses available to us. To me, this is what Foucault meant by daily responsibility to embrace "hyper and pessimistic activism" and make "the ethico-political choice" about "the main danger." Reading with sociological imagination, then, is both helpful and hopeful.

CHAPTER 4

Will I Still Read
in the 21st Century?

Depending on to whom you listen, the 21st century will mean the end of my reading or my awakening from the linear oppression of rational arguments coded in long printed tomes. Because of new media and their affordances, our access to print has become subordinated to image, and we are becoming inattentive, unable to concentrate, stupid, overstimulated, homogeneous, narcissistic, or a combination of these. Children are Vitamin D deficient and obese because they game continuously indoors. Adolescents are addicted to social networking, casting off media alternatives in order to find more efficient ways to narrate their lives in excruciating detail. Adults like me are irrelevant because we represent the past and the point is the here and now. Or . . . new media flattens the Earth; opens more portals for me to gather, create, and distribute meaning and entertainment; makes information free and fast; gives us time; and creates new forms of writing and reading. It's only that "the tradition of all the dead generations weighs like a nightmare on the brain of the living" (Marx, 1969, p. 15) that separates adults from children and youth . . . I don't own a cell phone, and I still can't spell.

We enjoy a week off between summer reading camp and the start of the fall semester. For the past several years, Kathleen and I have attended the SummerWorks Festival in Toronto. Over 10 days, 40 or so one-act plays are presented in four relatively small theater spaces along Queen Street. The festival provides aspiring playwrights, set designers, and professional actors with audiences and opportunities to demonstrate their talents. Last year's favorite was an hour-long story of social alienation told entirely through first-person narration using paper cutouts and colored transparencies on an overhead projector. The performance was riveting.

This year, Norman Yeung's *Theory* captured our imaginations. The theater for 100 with low-rise seating became assistant professor Isabelle's classroom for her course on film theory. (Although I had no lines, I want

George Clooney to play me, if the play travels to Hollywood.) Although I was positioned as a student, my attention was devoted to the teacher's praxis. Her theory was that expression should be free in film and society. Her pedagogy reflected this theory in two familiar ways. First, her students would participate in a class blog that hid participants' identities from each other and from the teacher, inviting candid communication, she hoped. Second, the class would take up controversial topics in films, showing how films work on serious topics of race (*Birth of a Nation*) and gender (*Baise moi*). Similar to my students, Isabelle's students resisted the inauthentic use of digital media and expressed concern that the films' topics positioned groups differently among their peers. Isabelle's quick interpretation that resistance equals a lack of seriousness was all too familiar to me as well.

Within the bulk of unengaged blog postings, one student began to splice class film clips with samples from his private viewing. (The content of the postings implied that this blogger was male.) Over time, his text increased in both his explicitness concerning the controversial topics and his technical expertise. At first, Isabelle was ambivalent about these texts—on the one hand, they were serious, but on the other, they offended class members. Despite student protest and the advice of her husband and department chair, Isabelle continued to support her original commitment to free expression. The blogger persisted and deepened his intentions to provoke, adding class images and hallway conversations between Isabelle and her husband, as well as bringing new media to his mix and messages. Seeing her image and words repositioned in his postings, Isabelle surrendered her theory.

After the play (no, I'm not going to explain the ending), Kathleen and I couldn't stop talking about a scene in which the anonymous blogger visited Isabelle during office hours to complement her on her pedagogy. He remarked that film critics in the 1980s worried needlessly that art and expertise would disappear with the advent of digital media tools because, clearly, that hadn't happened. Rather, the real danger of new media was/is that we are never unrecorded, and we cannot control or erase the meanings ascribed to our images and words. Both can be reconfigured and juxtaposed with other images and sounds, creating new meanings to be distributed for all who care to read them.

Theory challenged my thoughts about theory, new media, and reading as performed in this play. The apparently insurgent blogger considered himself to be Isabelle's ideal student in this class (that we shared with him). As she/we read his work, reason and emotions collided with each other, tapping into some of the more important issues of 21st-century literacies: privacy, surveillance, connectivity, authority, accessibility, multimodality, and originality. If I am to read and teach reading in the 21st century, then Isabelle's issues are mine as well.

PRIVACY/SURVEILLANCE/CONNECTIVITY

What I read has become how I'm known. It used to be that only my parents, teachers, and an occasional librarian cared or worried about my reading tastes and practices. They would recommend books, plays, art exhibits, films, and music that they knew would be "good for me" and hoped I'd like. Although at times predictable (everyone should read . . .), their suggestions were often surprising—Mildred King, a junior high librarian who seemed ancient, introduced me to Dave Brubeck's music because I wore thick glasses and a skinny black tie. After my rant during his high school history class about the British in Ireland, Arthur Brownell, a boring lecturer, gave me his copy of A. J. P. Taylor's *The Origins of the Second World War*, in which the author explains with apparent joy British culpability. And my father told me to visit the Rochester Art Gallery on weekends because "that's where girls will be." In retrospect, such intrusions into my private life were often interesting and beneficial, but they were rarely based on studied profiles of my preferences or actions. Rather than paying anything but cursory attention to me, the intruders shared a bit of their lives with me. And while I spent much of my youth and adolescence trying to fly under adult radar and the official curriculum, I still remember their attention.

Now, however, every time I read some text, someone somewhere catches me in the act. Not because they know that my reading is wrong (although certain texts are considered wrong) or that I am acting improperly (never mind), but because they learned some patterns about my choices. Buy two tickets to the Galileo exhibit at the Franklin Institute, and we're swamped with suggestions of other shows we're sure to like and of fund-raisers for Philadelphia arts. Visit "how to" websites to design and build a bathroom, and plumbing and bathroom supply addresses appear in my related column every time I jump on the Internet. Amazon.com peppers my inbox daily with notices about new books that I must read. Pandora.com sculpts my playlist. Google will sort my

Gmail into priority, starred, and everything-else categories, according to my opening/reading of previous emails. The list goes on.

Each attempt to read is measured, analyzed, and profiled, and then fed back to me as a service. Although this attention could be considered flattering and helpful, my reading choices and practices define me. And it's not just a matter of my using the Internet. Any time I visit the library, a bar, or school, my face and body are videotaped, and if I'm (un)lucky I could appear permanently on the Street View feature of Google Earth for those spots. The GPS in cars I rent enables the tracking of my movements. Foursquare and Facebook Place lets my friends check on my location at any time. Subscriptions put me on lists. Phone conversations are tapped by government officials and quality control experts and, were I a celebrity with a cell phone, are hacked by the audio equivalent of paparazzi. By seeking texts to read for whatever personal and private reason, I am creating a public and permanent record that is not in my control. The intruders into my personal and private space neither share parts of their lives with me nor care about what's "good for me" personally. I become a data point and a consumer.

Facebook founder Mark Zuckerberg thinks that I should get over myself, because privacy is no longer a social norm. "In the last 5 or 6 years . . . people have really gotten comfortable not only sharing more information and different kinds, but more openly and with more people" (as quoted in Johnson, 2010). His declaration followed his company's switch of its default setting from private to public, enabling Google and Microsoft to measure, analyze, and use all new information posted unless the individual adjusts his or her privacy settings. When Zuckerberg designed Facebook while a student at Harvard, he assumed privacy was valued, but he is proud of his company's role in privacy's evolution. "We view it as our role in the system to constantly be innovating and updating what our system is to reflect what the current social norms are" (as quoted in Johnson, 2010). Although it's probably obvious that I don't have a Facebook account, Zuckerberg's narration of the quick death of people's interest in privacy seems too simple to me. And it's not just because I'm old. (Many researchers dispute the charge that children and youth disdain privacy, by tracking their adjustment of Facebook privacy settings.)

Judge Richard Posner is famous for articulating Zuckerberg's position, arguing that privacy for individuals is an overrated social good with a very short history. He contends that privacy is lightly ingrained within the human psyche, culturally specific, and tied to political and economic privilege. As evidence, he cites the current practices of surrendering privacy for relatively little gain: We click online to purchase, we allow medical records to be digitized and kept on multiple servers, we buy E-Z Passes to zip by tollbooths, and we forfeit constitutional rights to prevent terrorist planning. If people valued their privacy as a fundamental right, he reasons, none of these practices would be popular or even possible. Posner frames privacy as concealment in which individuals hide information about themselves in order to gain advantage over others, projecting that they are healthier, wealthier, wiser, and more honest than they really are and therefore creating inefficiencies in the economy and government. Similar to Zuckerberg, Posner welcomes individual transparency in order to facilitate efficiencies in business and government, while defending business and government rights to privacy (concealment) because those institutions serve society more generally. Too early disclosure would stifle innovation and diplomatic negotiations, don't you know.

Although Aristotle made a distinction between the public sphere of commerce and political activity and the private sphere of family and home life, the modern version of legal protection of privacy was a response to modern communications technology—mass distributed newspapers and easily developed photography (Warren & Brandeis, 1890). Isabelle objected to the use of her image and words to achieve someone else's ends, lamenting the circulation of power over meaning and identity within her class as one student used information about her to make his point without her permission. The creation of profiles based on my reading practices places me in a similar position, and the sale and use of that information commodifies my reading (me) in a new way. It's not that my reading is cultural capital that I can choose to sell to others as an employee or subscriber; rather, my reading is repackaged in order to be sold back to me. More than annoying, I think it's dangerous.

Isabelle feared the possible physical violence in her reading of her student's blog entries. I worry about symbolic violence within this "evolving" of privacy in which my reading practices afford me a transparent rationalized life in order to provide efficiencies in commerce and governance. At once, my new life is permanent and independent of my control, although supposedly reflective of my true interests and preferences. Similar to Isabelle's dilemma, the inversion of my privacy is embedded in my modes of action and the structures of my thought, giving it at least the appearance of its legitimacy. That repackaged life, tailored to patterns in my reading practices, comes back to me stripped of its complexities and its tangents, honed to existing commodities, cutting me off from the reading practices and profiles of others. If I accept the offered position, diversity is slowly drained from my life as my circle of practices becomes narrower and narrower.

AUTHORITY/ACCESSIBILITY

I'll admit to having authority issues, but authority is central to my reading of Isabelle's dilemma. Because of her role, she enjoyed two of Max Weber's (1947/1997) types of authority, and she pursued a third type by the way she designed her class curriculum and pedagogy. Isabelle worked within an institution that afforded her (and me to be honest) the rational-legal authority of the state and the university's accrediting agencies. Through the formal rules of a professorship, she was granted control over students who desire to obtain a degree. Inside the classroom, she was in charge with legal and institutional recourse, if necessary, but outside that space, she had little legitimate authority over her students. Additionally as a teacher, Isabelle relied on the long-established customs and habits of traditional authority within the educational dyad—teacher and student. Although pedagogy styles might vary, teachers are ceded control over student deportment and outcomes in the relationship. Both these types of authority had little to do with Isabelle or her ideas or practices; rather, they stemmed from the role she performed.

At least in my reading of the play, Isabelle sought to transcend rational and traditional authority by the force of her intellect and presentation. She hoped to capture students' attention and imaginations by demonstrating the power within her readings of films, explaining the relationships between the ideas and lives they represented and the ideas and lives of her students. Coupled with her trust of their freedom to express themselves, she worked to command their learning through her charisma. She succeeded apparently with only one student because the rest of her class spoke only of the course requirements and the disturbing nature of the films, her readings, and that single student's postings. During the first face-to-face meeting between Isabelle and that student in her office, he evinced his acceptance of her charismatic authority through his effusive praise for her content and style. By that time, however, Isabelle was too shaken to consider the implications of his tribute, and she chose to retreat from charisma to her traditional, and then legal, powers. I think I understand her choices.

In the Happy Valley, we are experiencing what appears to be the slow death of our local news sources. What used to be a whack against our front door in the morning is now a noise too soft for me to hear. I must make a visual inspection to see if the newspaper has arrived for breakfast. Owned by the McClatchy Group (America's third largest newspaper chain), the *Centre Daily Times* produces approximately 12 pages daily of local-interest stories and sports with amateur community columnists and occasional syndicated op-ed pieces. Never the equivalent of "the paper of record," over the past 5 years, our *Times* has retreated from connecting our local stories with much happening beyond the county line. At times, stories pay some attention to state news, and each day, it includes half a page of national and international news briefs. Our local television news has also become myopic in its vision, going national only for the weather, the stock market, and sports. Our commercial radio stations are nationally programmed with little news to speak of. These traditional news authorities are being (have been) replaced by community members' instant access to 24/7/365 information sources available through whatever means of desktop, notebook, or hand-held technology.

The result is an information glut in which readers have access to more information than they can process, from more sources than ever before, and according to more authors and designers than in the past. My colleagues at work walk the halls equipped with more and more gadgetry that enables them to search for, capture, analyze, design, produce, and distribute information on most, if not all, topics within seconds. The lobbies of our buildings feature screens, blaring constantly "breaking news" from networks designed to keep all up to date on what's happening around the flat world. Supplementing these flows are blogs, websites, tweets, and outlets invented between this writing and the publishing of the book. With ever increasing access to our attention, the authors, designers, and reporters of these countless texts offer their representations of the world and all that's in it with varying degrees of rational, traditional, and charismatic authority. Readers are challenged to decide on which might be "good" authorities to help them translate information into knowledge in order to make or participate in decisions that affect their lives.

Here is where Isabelle's and my readings overlap. She questions the authority by which her student distributes his texts as if they were legitimate representations of film/life connections and as if he were a legitimate authority. His texts present assertions and provocations, but offer few visible warrants supporting his arguments. On their surface, then, the texts appear to be only bits of disturbing information that fill Isabelle's inbox. My metaphoric inbox is filled with texts from unknown sources providing me with information. These sources typically contend that their information provides me with advantages over others in our postindustrial, information-based world. One challenge to my reading is to perform information triage to determine which of the texts might help me. The rush of the texts toward me, however, mediate against any slow deliberation over my choices, and I am forced to act at if I were George Clooney on *ER*, developing 18-second diagnoses of which texts to save and which to let sit in my waiting room. (I use this metaphor just in case this book makes it to Hollywood.)

For better or worse, the disappearing news media in the Happy Valley used to comfort me that someone was vetting these representations of the world before they came to me. Networks, writers, fact checkers, and editors filtered the raw information for me in ways that garnered my trust and that of others in the community. Mistakes, distortions, and conflicts of interest were minimized through trustworthy intermediaries and corrected through public commentary in order to assemble, at least the working appearance of, a system of accountability. Less information from fewer sources kept the text flows manageable and varied enough, enabling me to organize the information according to my values, theories, and frames and to become knowledgeable enough about the world to make decisions about my life.

Although much of the current deluge of information still flows through some form of mediation (network and newspaper presence on the internet, Google and the like, even wikis restrict posting according to rules of access and content), there are the real-world equivalents of that student in Isabelle's class, who make it past the filters and by their own authority find access to a broader audience through various media. Perhaps amateurish in their abilities to represent the world when compared with established sources, these insurgents can provide different vantage points from which to view, to consider, and to frame events. Isabelle's student subverted her subversion of traditional film theory, implying that her theory of the freedom of expression was embedded in technologies of control and exposing the gatekeeping function, of perhaps all three of her types, of legitimate authority. His access to the class through the blog afforded all the students (and the audience) an opportunity to reconsider the meaning of "good" authority on the production of texts and ideas.

In a sense, many of us live permanently in multiple digital Libraries of Congress with possible access to any information we might desire, if we can figure out how to find it on the "shelves," determine its value to us, and harness it for our purposes. One danger, of course, is that we get lost in the "stacks," are overcome by compressions of time, hurrying our triage practices, and reach for the shiniest, most accessible texts. We have several famous 21st-century examples of otherwise intelligent people making decisions as if they were lost in these spaces (e.g., the Wall Street bailout, the Sherrod firing, or the White Sox signing Manny Ramirez for the 2010 stretch run). A second danger, the one that echoed after attending *Theory*, is to worry too soon about the legitimacy of the authority behind the texts we encounter without thoroughly considering how their perspectives could move our understandings. As Lemert reminds us, "We live in a time when life requires us to refrain from jumping too quickly to conclusions shaped by what we once believed to be good and true" (2008, p. x).

MULTIMODALITY/ORIGINALITY

The films and postings in Isabelle's class appeared only for moments on the screen at the back of the stage. The play's director used those texts as fleeting data to provide justifications for the characters' talk and actions. Five of that student's postings were shown periodically for less than 20 seconds each time. Yet any audience member could see the student's developing facility with the blog medium and his interest in layered messages. His first was a series of silent quick cuts among the course films, linking race and sex with short captions. Across time, he developed more sophisticated skills in feathering sounds, photographs, and color into and across segments of his text. All additions seemed intentional, making the text more explicit to and for readers, but particularly for Isabelle. His final text remixed film clips, photos, class print, strategically repeating images for emphasis, with sound overdubs from popular music, the films' soundtracks, students' classroom talk, and Isabelle's lectures, and apparently private conversations with her husband at school. Despite all these symbols or perhaps because of them, Isabelle and I didn't understand the student's original purpose for his texts until he visited Isabelle's office and explained his homage to her in so many words.

I'd like to blame my lack of insight on the brief exposures during the play or even my solidarity with a fellow professor, but I'm afraid it's more the result of a lack of understanding and appreciation for digital mash-up texts. Clearly, *Theory*'s playwright, director, and designer spent hours considering how to represent that student's development of these technical skills, but also operationalizing an array of identities that he would adopt temporarily during this progression. In a bit of cliché, the department head characterizes that student to Isabelle as someone experiencing difficulties during face-to-face communicating with his peers, as if digital communication was typically a substitute for "the real thing." To me, the playwright and director do a much better job with his postings than this slip in character development implies. Although I missed the big picture until told, I could see shifts in the student's identity from timid student to film critic to provocateur to author to teacher within his texts. In one sense, the play could be read as a tale of this student's sense of becoming and its consequences for others and him.

And in this regard, I slightly redeemed myself as a reader. Although I was slow to uptake his intended meaning for his texts, I was able to understand how the texts worked, what they did, and why they produced those effects. His assemblages of sights and sounds in motion on the screens, beaming and blaring, flaring and fading, and racing and resting, tripped my thoughts and emotions, slowly creating anxiety in Isabelle as well as in me. The multimodal nature of his texts provided him more tools to negotiate his becoming and his production of their effects. And the playwright and director's uses of multimedia afforded them more tools with which to make their play work on the audience. Consider simply the use of Isabelle's body. Her physical presence represented a hanger for professional clothes to signify her legal authority. The student's focus on parts of her body objectified Isabelle differently. His clips of her voice disembodied her, and toward the play's climax, her body became the screen for his postings symbolizing their impact on her (and the audience).

Multimodal symbols provided entry points for reading *Theory*. All seemed essential and none were privileged over another system.

Although I found the images to be stimulating and effective in making clear how the student's texts worked and the turmoil they produced, I needed his explanation in his voice to understand his point and point of view. His words turned my reading upside down and sent me back through the play's multiple texts to map the trajectories of his becoming as well as Isabelle's. In some small way, those maps represent my becoming a reader in the 21st century as well.

The content of those multimodal texts challenged my understanding of originality. Although all texts are intertextual, nearly every element from the student's texts was a recycled bit from some other source. The nuns at my elementary school called this practice copying at best (move my desk away from all others) or plagiarism at worst (throw my work in the trash can publicly, send me to the principal, and call my mother). Their voices rang in my ears as I thought about the tension between those often familiar elements and the student's new twist on their meaning. Little, if any, credit was given to the original sources, which seemed wrong to me until I began to wonder about the originality of the originals. The student who designed the texts, however, was not claiming that those elements were of his making. His originality was his appropriation of elements from the class texts that were already in play, and then his placement of them within a unique design in order to extend that area of play to ideas not yet considered. His texts, then, read as hypergraphic applications of Debord's (1970) Situationist statement about plagiarism in *The Society of the Spectacle*:

> Ideas improve. The meaning of words participates in the improvement. Plagiarism is necessary. Progress implies it. It embraces an author's phrase, makes sure of his expression, erases a false idea, and replaces it with a right one. (p. 207)

Debord implies that few texts are original as I initially conceived of it; rather, they are built from and with the ideas from other texts, providing us with maps of the ideas' routes in the process of becoming that text. With appropriated elements, hypergraphic texts represent their social origins explicitly, but in a manner different from the formal citation that I expected. The student's texts were to be read as detournement, subversions of the texts of origin and Isabelle's assembly of them in order to create a new situation in which everyday practices are disrupted, providing spaces in which new ones might be developed. I read similar intentions in the texts of cultural jammers—Adbusters, the Billboard Liberation Front, the Cacophony Society, Guerilla Girls, Sisters of Perpetual Indulgence, the Yes Men, and many others. But should I extend this reading to all the hypergraphic texts I encounter?

Outside such groups, many individuals actively engage with, re-work, and appropriate ideas and elements from texts in order to design and produce hypergraphic texts to communicate with, inform, and entertain others. Although access to hardware and application might vary, according to the Kaiser Family Foundation (2010), youth between the ages of 8 and 18 spend 7.5 hours a day using media (76% own mobile technologies with capabilities beyond speaking to another and spend a full 90 minutes texting daily). Many among this group and a significant percentage of adults choose to construct and distribute remixed hyper-graphic content broadly, which is often eagerly read by others, bounced back with comment, as well as passed on. Most make one or two stops, but some (many in comparison to traditional texts) become viral, circling the globe and adding to the inbox piles.

My box gets filled with two basic types of memes. Colleagues send me engaging hypergraphic texts that challenge mainstream media takes on current events or more likely the way the world works—Anne Leonard's "Story of Stuff" (2008) or RSA Animate production of David Harvey's lecture "Crises in Capitalism" (2010). Friends send me ones that they think are funny and reinterpret the seriousness of everyday life. While I understand the first type as postmodern representation of modernist arguments, I wonder about the time spent on the funny ones. Both types display a greater role for entertainment in communications; yet the latter type promotes play as a cultural value, if not a recovery of play as the basis of culture. With the exception of the ones involving kittens, each text invites me to read it as an original effort to appropriate from others in order to try on and negotiate new meanings and identities and to make spaces (places?) for some ideas or people in the world. I must read them in a manner similar to past authors and artists who've used recognizable imagery in order to shape my perceptions of the world and my place in it.

21ST-CENTURY SKILLS

In this light, how should I read the calls to harness these capacities of (for) text production as 21st-century skills? My focal hypergraphic text is a series of four You Tube videos titled "Did You Know/Shift Happens" (http://shifthappens.wikispaces.com). Originally created as a print-driven digital slide show for high school teachers in 2006, the first text is organized as a series of calls and responses, suggesting that the world is flat; other countries are poised to overtake the United States as the dominant world economic power; and Americans have been slow to adjust to the rapid transition to digital communications and their effects on work, our international standing, and our lives. Although intended to scare its audience, the original begins with an adolescent joke ("sometimes size does matter") that leads to an ominous cautionary tale of global competition in which China and India are stealing our language and jobs, and if we are not careful, sealing our fate to repeat the fall of England as the world power across the 20th century. At home, work is becoming unstable and unpredictable through competition and rapidly improving technologies, demanding that workers adapt to this compression of time and space in order to allow our businesses to compete. The last two slides draw the conclusion that "shift happens" and "now you know."

Uploaded 10 months later, Version 2.0 changed the background music, added graphics, rearranged the sequence of calls and responses, and cut the opening joke. International competition remains the central motivation and communications technology is still the solution (2.0 is still online). Curious among the calls is a reference to how advertisers might take advantage of the rise in social networking media. After the "Shift Happens" slide in 2.0, the text becomes explicit about what viewers should do now that they know, naming the skills of the 21st century. Students, workers—all people—must learn to remember, understand, apply, analyze, evaluate, create, communicate, and collaborate, if the United States is to keep pace with other nations. Viewers are told to advocate for these new skills among students, teachers, principals, school board members, and elected officials.

Version 3.0 arrived August 2008 with flash graphics, a greater color palette, and a dance beat sound track with the accents coordinated with each new call. International competition returned to the initial position of the original followed shortly by statistics attesting to the rapid changes in and unpredictability of the nature of work. At that point, "Shift Happens" spoke for the first time, with a female voice repeating, "Right Here! Right Now!" until the call turned toward ad space and media user statistics under the banner "a market share." For the first time, 3.0 provided space for product placement, couching it in humor (*BG* stands for

"before Google"). This version ends with a reference to illegal down-
loading of music, leaving 21st-century skills implicit, while asking explicitly, "So what does this all mean?"

In version 4.0 (Fall 2009), the designers answer their own question,
demonstrating that their improving skills of collaboratively creating hy-
pertexts can be put to commercial use. Under the same franchise name,
they abandon their original audience in order to speak directly to advertisers, explaining that print and broadcast media are dying from lack of
access and use, while the convergence of new digital technologies and
social networking are where the money is. Everything is getting faster,
smaller, and cheaper, "affecting the way people behave." The closing,
"Now that's convergence, and now you know" precedes a list of credits
(offered for the first time) and a notice for an upcoming Media Conver-
gences Convention sponsored by *The Economist* magazine.

I became aware of "Did You Know/Shift Happens" as the theme
for a National Council of Teachers of English conference in 2008. By
that time, the 2.0 YouTube had gone viral with 5 million hits. Version
4.0 had reached 20 million. Reading all four versions with social competence told me that the future is bleak for Americans in a flat world, it's
all about business and competition (particularly with East Asians), and
my only protection will be harnessing the skills I used previously to design hypergraphic texts for my purposes in order to gain an advantage
over others at and through employment. In the 21st century, I'll need to
move my social networking from play to work, the texts I produce from
detournement to recuperation, and myself from homo luden to homo
laborimus, and then homo emptor. Early versions called for school curricula to become digital in order to hone students' native and naive social
networking skills toward employment. Later versions explain how the
networks can deliver all users to market. "Shift Happens" demonstrates
this future through its content, its evolution of design, and its shift in audience. In the end, the designers are hobnobbing with the editors of the
conservative, pro-business *The Economist*. To me, the danger seems to be
that his "Shift" is the shaft.

I read "Shift Happens," in particular, and the concept of 21st-century
skills, in general, as modernist corrections to postmodernist practices of
reading. In *Theory*, readers were invited to seek meanings in textual representations of complex human relationships across multiple layers of
difference, to question assigned positions in the received world, and to
problematize power realized through technology. In "Shift Happens,"

however, technology and the science behind it lead necessarily to progress, making life easier for all and providing material benefits for everyone willing to embrace rationality and renounce emotionalism and parochialism. In order to guide us through the "Shift," the state and business will redirect our attention from the personal and idiosyncratic to the global and generalizable. Failure to read texts through these modernist assumptions will jeopardize our standard of living and doom citizens of developing countries to continue their failed traditions. Memories, understandings, appreciations, analyses, evaluations, creativities, communications, and collaborations are to serve instrumental goals.

Yet the struggle to perform reading in the 21st century is not simply between modern and postmodern iterations. Traditionalists continue to champion their values of history, place, family, faith, and community. For example, consider lamentations for the waning of social capital in the United States (e.g., David Brook's op-ed pieces three times a week in the *New York Times*) and perhaps around the world (e.g., Putnam, 2004). This is to say that my 21st-century encounters with texts will be mashups of traditional, modernist, and postmodern readings. The danger, it seems to me, is to think that one type of reading will supplant the others in time and space.

IMAGINING PEDAGOGY

"Who is Shirley Sherrod?" The incident surrounding Ms. Sherrod during the summer of 2010 served as the prompt to name and develop the practices of information triage and reading around a subject. Working in teams of five students, undergraduate students and I speculated on the institutional processes of informational triage, chose and pursued five associated topics around the incident, and then represented our new knowledge through the hypergraphic applications available on our notebook computers. Although there's enough in the incident to fill a semester, we worked within the time compression of education and devote one 3-hour session to this cause. In many ways, Ms. Sherrod's life is heroic, but it is tragic in the way that it became public knowledge. Reacting to a posting on a small conservative website and then FoxNews.com, federal officials required Ms. Sherrod to pull her car to the side of the road in order to text her resignation as Georgia state director of rural development for the U.S. Department of Agriculture (USDA).

Few of my 25 undergraduates were familiar with the incident, but all thought the officials' methods were "rude." All wondered what could prompt such action, particularly when it would become public knowledge within hours on the Internet. Within 15 minutes' work, groups assembled a time line from the posting of a 2-minute YouTube of Sherrod speaking before a state delegation of the National Association for the Advancement of Colored People (NAACP), her dismissal, and then a rush to apologize when the original posting was exposed as an inaccurate representation of Sherrod's speech and actions. The original posting portrayed Sherrod as a racist, failing to assist a White family about to lose their farm to foreclosure in 1986. The 45-minute speech and later testimony from the family suggested that the opposite was true. At the end of building the time line, one student asked, "Did the Obama administration learn nothing from the Louis Henry Gates affair?"

To address that question, we engaged in what Kate Atkinson (2008) calls "reading around a subject" in her novel *When Will There Be Good News?* It is the opposite of rushing to judgment by taking time to build a context for any event, topic, or idea. In our case, each student within a group selected one aspect of the incident to build that part of the context. Some selected basic elements: Who is Sherrod? What is FoxNews.com? The USDA? And the NAACP? Others thought historically: How does the USDA help farmers with foreclosure? Who gets such help? How did Sherrod get her position? And still others work politically: Why would Obama follow a Fox story? How does race figure into the administration's decision? Why is speed of the essence in 24/7 news cycles? This is the Internet at its most useful, gathering information; however, at the 20-minute check, we reported more than one position on several of the topics. We set three rules for information triage: you must be clear about your goals for gathering information ("Obama's officials were more interested in fending off criticism than getting at the real story"); you must have knowledge of the Internet and how to access all types of databases ("They didn't check with other possible sources away from the politicized 'news' of Fox News") and you must leave yourself time to sort through the information available ("They rushed to judgment, and were wrong. Obama is supposed to be deliberate. They should have been on this case").

The teams of five combine their triaged information gathered during their reading around the subject, and then together, they design original assemblages of "plagiarized" mash-ups presented in hypergraphic texts.

READING THEORY

"We are Borg. You will be assimilated. Your biological and technological distinctiveness will be added to ours. Your culture will adapt to service us. Resistance is futile."

These few sentences became the standard message of the invading force of cyborgs on the science fiction television show *Star Trek: The Next Generation*. The Borg "invited" other populations to join their management team as cyborgs with enhanced ocular and aural powers, improved strength, and a feed to a collective intelligent life force, making all members' lives carefree. With glasses as thick as the bottoms of Coke bottles, wireless access to the Internet, constant availability through email, and orthotics for falling arches in my basketball shoes, I believe that I have been assimilated, and technology meshes with my organic functioning. Knee replacements, pacemakers, sleep masks, cell phones, retinal implants, and the like allow me and my friends to joke about being Jamie Sommers or Steve Austin—the $6 million couple. We are cyborgs with technologies in our bodies as well as managing our everyday practices. Life and fiction combine, and resistance seems foolish as well as futile.

Yet *Star Trek* positions The Borg as insurgents, portraying resistance as noble, if difficult. We can read at least two centuries of concern about cyborgs, dating for me from Mary Shelley's *Frankenstein; or, The Modern Prometheus* (1818/2001) to Chris Hedges's *Empire of Illusion: The End of Literacy and the Triumph of Spectacle* (2009). Shelley read technology's interface with humans as a threat to human emotions and a misunderstanding of the complexities of humans in nature, and Hedges reads the intimate relations between people and communications technology as the conduit for irrationality and apathy as image supplants reality. Both argue that technology mediates our lives, simultaneously alienating us from ourselves and others and inveigling us to participate in order to make our lives easier. For them, technology is not Borg-like—an alien force. Its perils are not done to us, but something that we do to ourselves through our desires.

Beginning from different points of origin, Martin Heidegger (1954/1993), Herbert Marcuse (1964) and Michel Foucault (1975/1991) described our culpability in the technological structuring of our lives. That is, we choose technology, they argued, in order to objectify and order the forces in our lives, enabling us to get things done effectively and efficiently. In making those choices daily, however, we position ourselves, others, and nature as comparable, manipulable resources in the management of our lives, home, industry, and society. Although all acknowledge this dynamic, none accepts The Borg's bargain or its mantra: "Resistance is futile." Shelley tells us to love our creations, Hedges asks for us to puncture illusions and to confront reality, Heidegger cautions us to "listen, but not obey," Marcuse proposes that we become more fully conscious of ourselves as part of nature, and Foucault calls for hyper and pessimistic activism in making ethico-political choices about the main danger.

These forms of resistance require reading the complex texts of the 21st century with sociological imagination, imploring us to embrace technologies, but to be thoughtful about management, the collective, and objectifications. According to advocates for new literacy practices, the normalizing of hypergraphic texts and communications technologies in everyday life could make such reading more likely. Global connectivity provides wider access to difference in histories and values (New London Group, 1996). Understanding the intentional and ideological uses of multiple symbol systems in design of texts arms readers with new tools to deconstruct and reconstruct the choices in the production of texts (Knobel & Lankshear, 2007). Hypergraphic layouts provide readers with multiple points of entry, facilitating alternative paths and interpretations (Kress, 2009). And through the social networks, readers learn to consider what a text does (how it works) as well as what it means (Masny & Cole, 2009).

CHAPTER 5

Are My Readings Dangerous?

Although I have not mastered reading with sociological imagination, I claim agency through my approximations. I'm convinced that I do know enough to ask questions and to participate in the decisions that affect my life. I can slow down the flow of texts toward me through information triage in order to read around subjects of interest. I have some understandings of the practices of production, the public pedagogies, and ideological intentions in a wide array of institutional and private texts. I realize that those texts frame events and ideas for me and represent how they and I are expected to fit into assigned roles in the world. And I admit that I continue to read with social competence (I have credentials), can be bamboozled (I keep voting in national elections), and do consume popular culture (I own a pink Hello Kitty guitar), media (we subscribe to NPR), and expert opinion (I listen to scientists explain global warming). While this reading comforts me in ways that keep me choosing to be compliant, it discourages me from thinking about and acting upon the inequalities that I am tacitly supporting through that competence. The tensions between reading with social competence and sociological imagination are in my head. I feel new power from the latter, but I worry about Lemert's warning—"We live now in a time when life requires us to refrain from jumping too quickly to conclusions shaped by what we once believed to be true and good" (2008, p. x). Can readings with sociological imagination be dangerous inside and outside our classrooms?

At the tea store this morning, I heard an interview on NPR concerning an attempt to broker peace between the government and the Taliban in the Swat Valley of Pakistan. The chief negotiator for the government is an elder Islamic cleric who hopes to eliminate the violence that has disrupted life in the valley for approximately 10 years. The cleric is negotiating with his son-in-law, whom he characterizes as intolerant of Western ways. Chief among the issues of contention is the education of women and girls. According to the report, the son-in-law's group has destroyed scores of schools for females because schools are spreading obscenities by teaching women to read. Although this might seem an obvious read, the story bled into my thinking about censorship at home—where children's books about "gay penguins" raising a chick, Wikileaks uploads on the United States in Afghanistan, and Oprah's declaration that she won't eat hamburgers raise firestorms—and my automatic response that I am against censorship. I think all these thoughts are directly connected to one another through social continuums of fear and control.

The report triggered an immediate, negative response from me. Clearly, the closing of schools for females is wrong, because it attempts to control their lives while not similarly constraining males. The Taliban's official sanction of inequities between sexes cuts deeply into my understanding of justice, positioning the son-in-law and his group as atavistic villains who fear a world in which females are able to acquire ideas beyond their immediate circumstances. Their violent reaction to their fears made it easier for me to assume a higher ethical ground. I fussed about the report on the Swat Valley all the way to work, connecting it to the *Jyllands-Posten* Muhammad cartoon controversy that escalated into more than 100 deaths, bans of burkas in schools across parts of the European Union, and even my mother's association with the Susan B. Anthony House. Upon arrival at my office, I had convinced myself of the superiority of my social theories to the son-in-law's. I am against censorship.

COMPLICATIONS

My reading of this NPR story began to melt almost instantly, however, because my associations with the Pakistani negotiations would neither stop nor confirm my convictions uniformly. Thoughts of the Muhammad cartoon in Denmark raised a memory trace to Sean Delonas's cartoon of a policeman shooting a monkey and exclaiming to his partner that they'll have to find someone else to write the next economic stimulus bill for the United States. One reading of the cartoon could be that the bill is so poorly written that a monkey must have used the typewriter, but even that reading leads to the association of President Obama, a Black man, with a monkey. The cartoon was published in the *New York Post* and caused an immediate outcry of racism—no destruction of buildings or deaths, but direct calls for censorship. The ban on burkas—even mothers wearing burkas when meeting their children at the school door in the

Netherlands—evoked thoughts of dress codes in our local high schools. Boys cannot let their pants hang exposing their colorful boxer underwear and girls must refrain from wearing halter-tops. Students claim that their rights of expression are violated by this censorship of sexual representation. In our house, Susan B. was nearly a saint, but few heeded her warnings about intemperance.

This second wave of associations to the negotiations of peace in the Swat Valley complicated the issue of censorship for me. Although the Taliban seemed clearly wrong, a negative evaluation of those who called for censorship of racism in the newspapers, sexualized dress in schools, and giving free rein to alcohol consumption are not so clear to me. I guess I do fear racism and seek to control racists. I believe our society has made sex a commodity and is selling it to children. I understand this is wrong because it seems to lead males to commit violence against females. I live in a college town in which students and local bar owners invented "State Patrick's Day" as an excuse to begin drinking at dawn on a weekend when the Saint Patrick's Day holiday falls on a weekday. Its success is credited to social networking through Facebook, but the first one resulted in 50 students being admitted to the emergency room of the hospital for alcohol poisoning. The NPR story and its personal aftermath began to take over my entire day. Do I oppose or favor censorship? And my answer was, "Yes!"

FOR THE KIDS

I appear to justify censorship, if by its use we protect people from harm. Racism harms racial minorities and dehumanizes the racist. Sexualized dress endangers women and girls and, again, makes men inhumane. Unlimited consumption of alcohol injures drinkers and threatens the physical and economic welfare of the innocent. In these cases, censorship of some texts seems justified because we are protecting others from harm. Yet I'm certain that the son-in-law in the Swat Valley or the Chinese government or even the Texas Textbook Selection Committee believe that they are justified to act on their readings of situations because they represent a "we" who wish to protect Islamic females from secularism, Chinese citizens from commercialism, and Texas youth from Satan as he spoke through Thomas Jefferson. In these latter cases, I consider censorship to be wrong because the topics don't appear harmful in the same direct ways to me. But who should decide about whether censorship is legitimate, for whom, and by what criteria?

Such questions bothered my quick, assured reading of the negotiations in the Swat Valley because I engage, at least tacitly, in censorship as well. Although at times I detect inconsistencies in my practices and go about my merry way, my straddling of the censorship issue would not leave me in peace. My reading of censorship seemed to be an instance of drawing conclusions on what I once believed to be true and good. I opposed censorship as an abstract category, but I accepted censorship based on what now seem to be two questionable assumptions—an essential character of the groups I would protect and a dominant direct effects model across media. I find little support for either—even in my life. Take, for example, Neil Postman's (1982) eloquent argument for protecting children from the adult secrets in the content and commercialism of media. The premise is dear to my heart because who doesn't want to protect children, but the notion of censoring media content (either directly or through denial of access) falls apart on those two assumptions.

Channeling Rousseau, Postman projects a natural innocence in youth which can be (has been) corrupted through too early exposure to the complexities of adult life before children are cognitively and emotionally ready to deal with them. In this process, children lose their innocence, are stymied in their development because they play less, and are commodified in the process. Postman argued that new media make too few demands on viewers, providing children with a steady flow of the seamier side of adult life and inviting them to act accordingly. Sexting among preadolescents makes his point, I think. But he'd probably point to children's ownership of cell phones as evidence as well. On its face, then, his argument for censorship appears worthy. Adults should censor commercial media in order to protect children.

Yet, to make his argument, he projects the essential category, childhood, in order to form his threatened group. Similar to many others, Postman ties the origin of childhood (children and youth ages 8 through 16) to the invention of the printing press. Prior to that date, he asserts, 8-year-olds were treated as (weak) adults, working in household economies, participating in any conversation, and engaging in adult entertainments. Starting in the 17th century, a growing percentage of families began to separate children from adults by encoding adult secrets within printed texts that required considerable teaching for children to gain access. He offers the development and growing popularity of public schooling until the mid 20th century as evidence of adults' intent to segregate themselves from the young. Although this seems plausible, even my family's experiences challenge Postman's universal category of childhood. My father and his 17 brothers and sisters (see Catholicism) started full-time work at or before the completion of primary school. They were filled with delicious stories about their introduction to the adult world during their first jobs in lumber camps, on farms, in households, and in factories. In the United States, child labor laws became federal in 1938, and they still exclude some farmwork to this day. Across cultures, classes, and genders, then, there are children to be sure, but not a uniform childhood to be preserved—even legally. (Think of the recent controversy over the definitions of childhood/womanhood at the Yearn for Zion Ranch in Texas.)

Postman's case also rests on a direct media effect model—the notion that media transfer designers' messages to a child audience. Even the youngest viewers, however, are selective in their attention around media; and therefore, they construct messages rather than accept them as presented. Moreover, that selective attention seems often to be intentional, demonstrating that children use media for their own interests, which are not always aligned with those of designers, authors, or other readers of the texts. Children are media users, not simply consumers of it. The messages that Postman feared are not simply imprinted on children's minds in a singular and linear fashion through exposure to various media. And my struggles to protect my children from sex and violence should have taught me this lesson long ago. Laura piled naked Barbies with uncombed hair in a corner of her room with little regard for Mattel's accessories or even Ken. While attending a Quaker elementary school, Tim Pat wrote war story after war story across American history in order to gain access to his older sister's play based on *American Girl* stories. In such light, censors always underestimate the capacities of those who are to be protected from harm. My kids never learned to accept my definition of media harm.

Such criticisms push hard against the terms I use to justify censorship —*protection, harm,* and *we*. If people, even children, can't be so easily corralled into essential groups, and they construct meanings according to their intentions and interests, then does any form of censorship make sense for any group? Is protection from information necessary in order to keep anyone out of harm's away? What does harm mean in these conditions? Who are the *we*, if we can't identify the *they*?

My original plans for my workday in tatters, I headed home with some temporary resolution to the puzzle that began with the NPR report on the Swat Valley in Pakistan. The world is too complex to supply an easy answer to the question, Am I for or against censorship? While it can be read as justified, it can also be read as paternalistic and patriarchal. And it is rarely successful. Censorship can't stop Pakistani girls and women from thinking and working to better their lives (however they define better). It doesn't protect anyone from racism, blasphemy, sexualized commodities, or even dangerous drinking. (College students drank to excess even during Prohibition in the United States—I know this from my mother's stories about how she met my father.) These differences among thoughts, beliefs, and actions exist despite efforts to censor and control them, and apparently, they find an infinite number of ways to manifest themselves—many too subtle for me to notice. Perhaps more useful questions about censorship, at least for me, are, Why does it exist and how does it work? I thought trying to answer these questions might make my readings around censorship less dangerous.

ANOTHER DAY

I hoped that NPR would air another story that would help me sort my way through my new thoughts about censorship, draining some of the potential danger from my readings of social things. And perhaps in an odd way, it did. With an apparent smirk to his tone, the radio host offered a brief report that the Vatican's semiofficial newspaper had published a longish article titled "The Washing Machine and Women's Liberation: Put in the Detergent, Close the Lid, and Relax." It explained how labor-saving technology had freed women from household drudgery in the West and would do the same eventually for women in developing countries. The subtext, for me, was that the other labor-saving technology, the birth control pill, which offers women greater control over their bodies, did not, and cannot, liberate women anywhere.

Although not identical to the son-in-law's position from the day before, the Vatican newspaper offered a reading of normal life and the future intended to control women in some ways that it does not seek to constrain men. The Vatican's version of normal life seems to offer women and girls more options than the Taliban; however, ultimately, it still rests on the fear of a world with knowledgeable females making choices for themselves, and it works aggressively to control what can and cannot be thought, said, or done in order to prevent that feared world from coming into existence. Before I caught myself, I was sliding toward quick conclusions about the censor and the censored. I had to force myself to think about how and why, rather than what and when, in order to avoid the danger of my reading the day before.

Control is the crux of censorship. It is a social act to deny a topic or practice. Censors' ultimate goal is to teach people to shun the censored topic or practice, diminishing the need for external social policing. Until that internal monitor is complete, however, the work of censorship is daunting and endless. On the surface, censorship appears to be a form of silencing, in which groups are denied certain information, and therefore, are unable to speak about the topic in any way. Certainly since 1968, when the pope issued an edict against the pill (which a new pope reconfirmed on its 40th anniversary in October 2008), the Vatican has withheld information from Catholic women and non-Catholic women who use Catholic institutions. Moreover, the Church sanctions any Catholic worker who attempts to subvert the pope's edict.

Yet in order to invoke and maintain the "silence," the Church, and therefore the faithful, must engage in two discourses continuously until the goal of internal personal monitoring is achieved. First, the Church must construct and maintain an apparatus to enforce the faithful's fidelity to the edict and to punish those who transgress. In order to construct these systems, it sponsors conversation about the pill and how to stop its use. Against its ultimate goal, then, this talk keeps the censored topic in the mouths and minds of the censors and those who are to be protected. Second, in order to encourage the transfer from external to internal monitoring, the Church must develop believable narratives to justify its position and consequent acts, by positioning the pill and the women who use it as outside the bounds of normal life. The central Vatican narrative is that the pill negates the intimate truth of conjugal love with which the divine gift of life is communicated. That is, the pill stops God's will. An additional narrative, the one reported by NPR, maintains that women's development is achieved through technology that enables their leisure. Accordingly, women don't really need the pill to better their lives, and they would be selfish to insist on it. A third narrative spoke to men from the same newspaper—the pill harms nature and men. The president of the International Federation of Catholic Medical Associations stated that the pill caused environmental pollution and male impotency. Combining these narratives, the pill is evil; unnecessary; and hazardous to nature, men, and God.

I don't mean to make light of censorship or how it works with this example. Many Catholics reject the pill in order to remain in good standing with the Church. Many Muslims are faithful to the son-in-law's version of Islam as well. Although the Catholic approach to censorship is now less physically violent, both adopt(ed) censorship as a tactic to bring their vision of normal life to reality, attempting to control others' views and lives, until the faithful (and all others) choose to embrace that vision as their own. Censorship is a means to accomplish that goal—complete with an infrastructure to enforce their vision socially until individuals choose to construct personal monitoring systems. To justify these actions, both construct and adapt narratives to invite that personal commitment to their vision. I find this reading of censorship less dangerous than my previous one because I've learned that censorship doesn't work, and I think the practices that surround it could provide more citizens access to decision making about their lives.

By giving in to fear and working to control, censors achieve the opposite results—they keep the topic or practice alive during their planning and implementation of their apparatus and narratives of control. Their talk and action invoke resistance from those producing and practicing the objectionable information or action, those who oppose censorship as a violation of free speech, and perhaps, many members of groups to be protected, who seek to choose for themselves. Resistance must be planned and coordinated through talk and social networking as well. Apparatus must be harnessed or developed to subvert the censor's approach, and narratives must be produced and distributed to counter the censors' visions of normalcy. According to my new reading, rather than quieting or denying, censorship sews the seeds to defeat itself, providing venues to discuss different visions of normal life in public.

Censors (me—yesterday) seek consensus—a collapse of these different visions into a single position—through the transfer of social to personal systems of control. Yet in the process their worst fears are realized because "the abnormal" remains in play before a much larger public audience. Reading censorship with this sociological imagination helps us understand that calls for censorship are invitations to discuss difference by challenging other people's views of what should come into being and for demanding respect for one's own views from other people. If practices of censorship can't bring consensus, then why not abandon it for tactics that might bring dissensus—a process of naming and clarifying those differences of all types and placing them in relationships to each other. We would work toward collective explanations of how people differ, where their differences come from, and how we can live and work together with these differences. Censors should realize that this might be their best chance to live their normal lives—by understanding and supporting others to live their normal lives as well. Perhaps it is a utopian goal to think that we can discuss and find ways to support differences, but in a connected world, it seems worth imagining ways to act and the efforts necessary to begin and continue.

WHY CAN'T THEY SEE IT?

At 60, people start to talk to you about retirement. When will it be, what will you do, and where might you do it? My concern, like that of so many others, is how? How will I survive after Penn State stops paying me monthly? With only a brief 3-year gap when I taught in Canada, the government has withheld Social Security taxes with the promise that they will send me checks after I retire. I find comfort in this promise and recognize how valuable this income has been to older relatives of mine. I know that not everyone participates in the system, but for most Americans Social Security income figures into their vision of a normal life after retirement. Since 1935, when it was enacted in the United States, advocates have worried about the solvency of the program. The current concern is, with all baby boomers retiring, will there be enough in reserve and incoming taxes to honor the promises? Young workers (Laura and Tim Pat) will have to support this bubble in the system.

One suggestion to ensure solvency is to privatize Social Security by requiring participants to invest their Social Security taxes within financial markets to keep pace with the economy. "Let the free market solve this problem," some Social Security experts and financial analysts report through radio, newspapers, televisions, websites, and blogs. Watching financial bubble after bubble burst on this market over the past 4 decades, however, I wonder why anyone would think this solution to be in their best interests, because the current rates of interest accrual would transfer to managers' fees as retirees ride up and then, most assuredly, down the financial market waves. Channeling my father's voice, I yell at the speaker, the page, or the screens, "Can't you see it? They took your paycheck (income rates for most Americans have been stagnant or fallen since the 1980s), your house (foreclosure rates hit historic highs and home values have tanked in many places), and now they want your retirement! Can't you see it? Why won't you act in your own best interest and block this idea from public discourse before it starts to sound like the only solution."

Why can't citizens read these media representations of retirement with a sociological imagination, ensuring a social safety net so that all can live healthy lives and feed themselves with a roof over their heads? My growing understanding of reading, however, demonstrates the danger in my rant and quick reading of the situation. I assume an essential character among American citizens that I first learned to do at home, and then, that I theorized during too many years of formal schooling—working people share an identity that binds us together in order to secure the conditions that will enable us to fulfill our rich human needs to be freely active, to affirm ourselves, to be spontaneous in our activities, and to pursue the free development of our physical and mental energies. Once secured, my narrative continues, we'll live normal lives—the ones that people were meant to live. This is my ultimate "it" that I wanted the "you" to see during my periodic rants. It frames my reading of social security and my readings around that topic. And it makes those readings dangerous for others and for me.

To discuss differences means that I must give up my notion of how people ought to read this or other texts in order to attempt to understand how others do use them and how the texts work for them as well as on them. Readers bring their discourses and narratives to bear on the various frames and representations of social security and normal retirement. They enter these texts from points of reference different from mine, and they want recognition for their approaches. For example, some women might take up the market possibility as a means to compensate for the government's calculation of survivor benefits, some minority workers could begin with their historical exclusion from jobs that provided Social Security possibilities or "retirement," some young people looking for work might ignore the frame or even Social Security as irrelevant and some readers could understand care during old age as a private family matter. In these cases, gender, race, age, and duty mediate the readings of Social Security, to say nothing of how a recently unemployed, 40-year old, Muslim, Black woman might engage these texts.

None of these readings trumps all others, and all are fully conscious of their perspective. Recognition of all readings as reasonable does not preclude the pursuit of any position. What recognition does is affirm the reading and the reader and invite participation into discussions of differences. To a limited extent, the media provide forums in which alternative readings and recognition can be made public. NPR served that function on my ride home from Grinnell, offering at least two expert points of view on many stories during its talk show formats. Often hourly news briefings were followed by longer investigations into how different interpretations of the events were possible. Television has its versions of recognition of difference on PBS, network Sunday morning, and literally endless talk on 24/7/365 cable news channels. Over the past several decades, newspapers have invented, managed, and watched the decline of op-ed pages designed to make different views public. And with modest expense, anyone can post on the Internet.

Despite these opportunities, many positions are rarely presented publicly or considered carefully, because of relative power and money behind the positions—think of the Spring Creek Canyon debate in the Happy Valley—and the concentration of ownership of media among a few corporate conglomerates—remember Disney brought you the Little League World Series Produced by Kellogg's Frosted Flakes Reduced Sugar. Within this context, editors and producers decide which issues to consider, how to frame and represent the issues, and who will appear within those frames and representations. The fact that these groups must compete to deliver an audience for advertisers produces spectacles of debate without much recognition of difference or chance for dissensus. On television, Glenn Beck's chalkboard is countered by Keith Olbermann's Worst Persons in the World. In newspapers, Paul Krugman's progressivism balances David Brooks's neoconservatism. On radio, Rush Limbaugh's Tea Party patriots oppose Pacifica's Free Speech Radio News listeners. To parody all this, *The Daily Show*'s video clips are challenged on *The Colbert Report* rants. These spectacles isolate groups and differences from one another, deny recognition to alternative readings and readers, and call for consensus around a single vision of normal.

Let me be clear, most of these decisions are made primarily to position readers as consumers of sponsors' goods and services as efficiently as possible. That's the business of media. Yet the content of these texts also positions their audiences, demanding that audience members arrange their multiple identities according to its frame, representations, and underlying discourse. The spokespeople for this content work to marshal evidence in order to legitimize the projected position, the rejection of alternatives, and the profit-making spectacle as natural and normal. In this process, the spokespeople and professional readers of these texts (pundits) comment often on the accuracy of the competitors' evidence, as if it will sway the public's willingness to accept the positions offered to them. If a frame or representation could be demonstrated to be inaccurate, critics reason, that reading of the social thing should be discredited (censored), and anyone who continues to choose its projected position should be considered a dupe. Truthiness, anyone?

Although understandable, this reading of the spectacle seems dangerous to me because it polarizes differences rather than offers any chance of dissensus. It locks others into a single essential identity, denies their readings of the situation as possible, and invites their resistance. To me, this reading for accuracy cannot lead to understandings of how people differ, where differences come from, and how we can live and work together with differences. Critics might feel better, but have accomplished little. Moreover, it assumes a direct effects model for media in which the spokespeople transfer intended messages exactly to the minds, mouths, and hands of its audience, neglecting how these frames and representations work as texts and how (and perhaps why) the audiences find them useful. Denying the agencies of others is akin to the work of censors, who seek consensus only on their terms. Although I do not favor calculated distortion, I do understand theory and value-laden perceptions of social things, and I don't think abstract discussions of accuracy will develop appreciation for multiple views of normal that are necessary for a democracy.

A LITTLE OFF THE SIDES

Russell charges me a finder's fee when I get my haircut. It didn't use to be that way. When I first walked into his barbershop (which he calls a salon) during my second month in the Happy Valley, he joked that he might need hedge clippers to transform the English garden on my head into a French one. The shop had four stylists, and he was clearly in charge with the first chair on the left. I'd wandered past three shops before I stuck my head in his door, making a tacit decision. He cut my head as we talked about the town; he told me about his experience; and we joked about my inability to sit still in the chair (razors, clippers, ears, nose, no glasses on, it's a struggle . . .). When I returned to my office, my colleagues made two comments. The first complimented my new French garden, and the second: "What did you have to talk about? He's a Dittohead."

When I thought about it, I could see their point. Although the signs have changed over time in his shop, they appear to be the opposite of the ones that surround me in my office. When he faces you toward his mirror, where Ronald Reagan once hung, now Sarah Palin thanks Russell for his contribution. Rush's peppered-analyses of events have given way to O'Reilly reports. Dean Martin has ceded the background to Michael Buble. Russell's "God bless you" remains sincere, and he speaks more often and openly about his fundamentalist faith. His nostalgia is also more pronounced than it was in the past as he wonders "why people just don't get it anymore." My office door has a poster for national single payer health insurance (different from the one I had in the early 1990s), and (still) has a copy of a 1907 newspaper article reporting that my grandfather "Babe" Shannon used an ax and his tree-climbing spikes to kill a 400-pound black bear that treed him while he worked in the woods of Upstate New York (it's to keep students at bay). Inside, I have a poster that I pulled off a London mailbox that proclaims, "Capitalism in crisis/Marx was right/socialism 2008"; another that reads, "Art is not a mirror held up to reality, but a hammer with which to shape it"; and many prints depicting people reading. What could we have to say to one another? Our answer is, "Plenty!"

The signs with which we surround ourselves represent identities with which we signal our memberships and affinities to others. As my colleagues recognized, Russell and I appear to have little in common. His Tea Partiers object to my socialists' taking their freedoms; and my socialists spot a few obscenely rich financiers and business owners with their hands on the strings controlling his partiers. From a distant vantage point, all that is visible is our oppositional queries—my "can't you see it?" and his "why don't people get it anymore." Those "its" represent different discourses with competing values that we use separately as the ideals against which to judge the merits of others' reasoning, ideas, and actions. And when we judge according to our "its," we follow carefully the socially constructed rules of fairness in our discourses. Typically, we would police the boundaries of our group, making sure that others see those barriers and none shall pass but true believers. When others read our signs, they should know what to expect and act accordingly. Russell and I should judge each other harshly and have little of consequence to talk about.

When I read our periodic encounters over the years, however, I see that we have not been typical, finding ways to achieve dissensus on a personal scale. Rather than beginning with the abstract values of our discourses, Russell and I started with the premise that we must share some principles that guide us. We discovered these shared principles within our talk of family, food, community, and work. Russell has seen my family grow older, because from time to time he has cut Laura's, Tim Pat's and Kathleen's hair. He has great skill with the tools of his trade. I have watched his family photographs change and multiply across these years. I accept his explanation that divine intervention led to his reunion with an estranged daughter as a special case for my materialism, and he acknowledges the special case of the need for a social safety net when we discuss our 95-year-old mothers. Currently, we are trading special pleadings as I see the strength he draws from his church after the Great Recession forced his son's business into bankruptcy and Bank of America foreclosed on his son's house and perhaps on Russell's as well in the process. And he wishes that the federal government would do something to protect them both as small businesspeople. Across discussions of family, we name some of our differences, note their origin, and explore how they could coexist.

I like to drink and eat, and Russell makes wine and loves to cook. Although we have never had a meal together, we talk often about food and agriculture. I live in town near three grocery stores, and Russell lives in a rural part of the Happy Valley (in a place called Zion—I'm not kidding) and has a quarter-acre garden. Our talk around these topics yielded a quick point of agreement—to buy local. We have different points of entry, however, for our shared position. Russell sees it as good business, and I see it as food safety—knowing how the food was produced and how far it's traveled—free market versus local regulation. We're negotiating on two related issues. Spring Creek is part of the Chesapeake Bay Watershed, and new environmental regulations restrict farmers' uses of some pesticides in our area. Russell worries that this will make farming more expensive, forcing more families to sell their farms. Although I share this worry, Tim Pat's work on the scarcity of clean water encourages me to support such efforts. Second, when we discuss food and local farming invariably we talk about the weather—drought, rain, and . . . climate change. We are still miles apart on this one, but we have discussed the Evangelical Call to Action on Climate Change.

As I read Russell, I realize that he demonstrates his commitment to a diverse community through who he has invited to work with him.

Stylists come and go, but they are/were never reproductions of himself in appearance, talent, or conviction (at least as far as I've known them). Charles died of AIDS during my third year of haircuts (Russell paid for his hospice care). Ronnie spent a year at the shop, and then Russell helped him establish the first African American barbershop in the Happy Valley. Marion worked for 6 years, brought her sister in as a Saturday colorist, and then left when Russell started to supply wigs for kids with cancer "because it's just too depressing." Susie is a refugee from Vietnam who is blind in one eye and came to the shop straight from beauty school. Russell is paying for her to fly to specialized trainings, grooming her to take over the business if and when he decides to retire. (I will start to shave off what little is left on that day.) If I asked Russell, I'm certain he would label this commitment to others Christian charity, but my term for it is *reading toward democracy.*

If everything is dangerous to and for someone(s), during some times, and in some places, my reading with sociological imagination has no absolute foundation on which I can stand. I become a main danger to myself and to the possibilities of democracy when I insist on the abstract correctness of discourses behind my framing and representations of reality in order to position others as out of touch, cranks, oppressors, or just plain wrong without bothering to imagine why they make choices concerning the main danger that are different from mine. When I engage in such acts, of course, I undermine the notion of reading with sociological imagination because I fail to question my frames and representations in my attempt to name and control their frames and representations. Rather, in these circumstances, I read to maintain social competence within my discourse group(s) as if it (they) were separable from all others, and I fail to imagine the possibilities of multiple views of normal lives learning to live and work together and I affirm the unsustainable status quo. In the end, I treat others as consumers of the truth of my knowledge and expertise.

Reading people (including myself) as open texts, however, offers the potential to locate commonalities within our lived experiences behind abstract values of our separate discourses. With that act, I imagine a space in which we could recognize invitations to discuss our differences concerning acts of censorship and control, the antidemocratic interests behind the media's representations of different groups, and inclusive democratic possibilities of dissensus. This form of agency requires willingness and the ability to shuffle creatively our multiple discourses in efforts to discover connections that could develop into coalitions, to produce further

actions and policies, and to invent inclusive ways to work and live together with our differences—to find ways that other narratives of normal
life and my narratives can be retained and restructured into our narratives of normal lives. And dangers lurk here too, I'm certain.

IMAGINING PEDAGOGY

We begin our talk about reading teachers drawing conclusions from data
by declaring our favorite medical shows on television. Everyone has
one, although not all are able to watch regularly and welcome Tivo, Net-
flix, and online streaming. The medical dramatic arc of illness, diagnosis,
cure, and resolution is made for 60 minutes (with commercial spots for
marketing drugs and insurance). All admit that American society has a
fetish for doctoring. After we dispute the authenticity of other's favorites
(whether or not *Nurse Jackie*'s sass would be tolerated, *Grey's Anatomy*
work schedules could be that open, or plastic surgery could be as preva-
lent as portrayed on *Nip/Tuck*), we settle down to discuss the representations of diagnosis and remediation in this genre. For dramatic effect,
television doctors sometimes misdiagnose early in episodes, and then
use data from lab tests and brilliant intuition to save the patient. *House* is
the archetype for this.

   Such representations make housecalls at schools because of the federal, state, and philanthropist/business insistence that data drive school
decision making in order to reform and improve student outcomes.
Many in class bristle at the notion that education tests possess validity and accuracy equivalent to a blood test, MRI, or colonoscopy. "Our
data are not as good," they deflect, implying that with better tests, teachers could reform and improve. They are surprised when I interject some
of Jerome Groopman's (2007) concerns about doctors' diagnosis and
treatment. A physician who teaches at Harvard, Groopman reports that
doctors begin assessing your health the moment they see you, tend to
interrupt patients within 12 seconds of the description of symptoms, and
arrive at a working diagnosis within 20 seconds. These snap judgments
arise, Groopman argues, because doctors are human and their thinking
is flawed. They diagnose by availability (what comes quickly to their
minds), confirmation bias (choosing among symptoms and test results),
and a host of questionable practices. Groopman concludes that the first
diagnoses persist, gain momentum, and are likely to be wrong. In order

to reduce diagnostic and treatment errors, while continuing the flow of patients, hospitals and HMOs require doctors to use standard heuristic flowcharts in order to reach their conclusions. "Your shoulder hurts?" "Yes." "Does it hurt to the touch?" . . . While useful in ordinary cases, Groopman maintains that these scripts reduce patients to objects.

Open the floodgates. Not lost in the personal stories about doctors, commercial influences, and doctor-proof materials are concerns about snap judgments, their persistence and their likely consequences in the classroom. Our subsequent talk considers the complexities of expertise and the possibilities of its arrogant expression when the test data, and not our personal knowledge of the reader, become the primary basis of our decision-making.

READING THEORY

All readers are biased. As Lemert warns, we must be on guard against too quick conclusions based on our certainties or we will affirm structures and discourses designed to suppress the differences among us. This challenges readers to be reflexive in their readings, and I'll admit that I find the challenge and practice behind it overwhelming at times. I know that naming my biases, as postpositivists advise (Phillips & Burbules, 2000), and situating them among others, are not adequate to meet this challenge. I can still be a closed text and privilege my point of view over others' even after I confess. I'm not convinced of Zygmunt Bauman's (2000) analysis that prescribed roles and identities have collapsed more or less completely, allowing me to self-consciously construct my own identity. Social structures are changing, to be sure, but I am not free of their influences (Foucault, 1975/1991). Perhaps the best I can attempt at this point is to adapt Pierre Bourdieu and Loïc Wacquaint's *Invitation to Reflexive Sociology* (1994) in order to use the tools of reading with sociological imagination on my attempts to read with sociological imagination. Although it is unlikely that this process will completely free me from bias while reading (McRobbie, 2002), reflexivity of this sort could provide a process through which to heed Lemert's warning continuously.

What might this mean? I must read my readings and me as texts with the intent and strategies to teach and position others as consumers of my point of view. I frame my texts and represent my version of normal life accordingly, making choices in the process of reading that are intended to enable the agency of my allies and to keep others from participating in decisions that will affect our lives. I am as effective in these practices as my relative power will permit within the mixing of traditional, modern, and postmodern contexts of my everyday life. And I am as dangerous as the other texts that surround me. The practices of reading with sociological imagination and the practitioners must be read with these tools in order to guard against reified points of view that objectify others, the swap of one view of normal life for another, and denial of the possibilities of dissensus.

As I've described them, censorship and control of others stem from our inabilities to live the sociological life as Lemert suggests—"to learn to accept things as they come down, then to imagine why they are what they are" (2008, p. x). Throughout the book, I've interpreted the latter part of this definition as reading with sociological imagination, and I returned to the first proposition in this chapter. During the last half century, what have come down are two destabilizing forces—different groups striving for recognition and redistribution of resources within the modern world and the compression of time and space in globalized capitalism (Peet, 2007). Although these forces are dislocating for all, censors cannot accept some consequences of these forces as they've come down and therefore seek to buttress traditional or modern structures of exclusion of differences through physical and symbolic means, controlling others' agency and access to decision-making in order to maintain some semblance of their previous power. Through metaphor, I've tried to demonstrate the futility of censorship without denying the violence of its practices. Race, gender, sexuality, ableness, class, locality, and a host of other identities and their combinations push against many traditional and modern views of normality and participation, denying the single common definitions imposed for so long in order to forestall Hobbes's war of all against all (Lemert, 2004).

If reading with sociological imagination can be an open set of reflexive practices (as I've imagined them in this and previous chapters), I see it as a useful means for censors and opponents of censorship alike. It helps us to address the questions, If the (my) world is different (filled with differences, not deficits, and global), then who am I? and How do I learn to be newly competent? Building on the notions of multiple identities, identity shuffling, and continuous identity construction (Fraser, 2000), I seek to find bridges across difference through the contextual negotiation of "talk" to find common values that could guide us toward dissensus.

CHAPTER 6

Who Reads Like This?

READING THEORY

I began this book with the declarations that I am not pessimistic about the present or the future, I don't think that we are fools as Frank Rich and others portray us, and I pin my hopes on reading toward democracy. I believe that democracy signals the possibilities of politics—that human needs can be addressed within communities. However in the United States, democracy is a tough read: If democracy implies the enfranchisement of all, why do so few vote; if it implies equal rights, why are some groups denied the rights that others enjoy; if democracy relies on access to information, why do so few own the media; if it implies "by the people," why such antigovernment sentiments; if democracy promises freedom, why do we practice censorship and surveillance; if it is the best political system, why must we export it through force; and if democracy has failed on its traditional promises of equality, civic participation, and freedom, why should we read toward democracy?

We can begin to address these questions by finding new ways to harness the agonistic potentials of liberalism and democracy. Traditionally, Western liberalism defines citizenship as a contractual relationship between each individual with the state, trading some of his or her vulnerable, but desired, freedoms for protected rights. "The great and chief end, therefore of men uniting into commonwealths, and putting themselves under government, is the preservation of their property" (Locke, 1689/1986, Ch. 9, para. 124). In this contract, each citizen is assumed to possess a stable, fixed identity and to be autonomous, rational, and self-interested. In order to preserve his or her life, freedoms, and valuables, then, a citizen chooses to establish the state as a neutral arbiter of disputes that will arise among interests. To ensure that his or her interests are included, the contract provides equitable ways in which each can participate in the identification of norms, rules, and laws intended to promote the common good. Those means become the political practices within the various forms of democratic government. The citizens and the state enable and control each other, ensuring both individual freedom and equality of rights as dynamic forces.

As I've tried to articulate across these chapters, liberal theory does not explain the conditions of our contemporary democracy (and it never has explained the actual conditions of any democracy). We cannot be confident in a single stable common good or a neutral government. Rather, we are blessed with a pluralism that cannot be easily papered over by "the common good" without the suppression of the interests and rights of some groups. Moreover, since each person belongs to numerous overlapping groups with multiple intersecting identities, which are neither singular nor fixed (Butler, 1993: Fraser, 1996), theorizing the common good requires the imposition of consensus concerning a normal life on all of us. In order to achieve that broad consensus, democratic governments have been only too willing to sacrifice the interests of diverse groups. As Chantal Mouffe (1996) laments, the imposition of consensus is a main danger.

> Pluralism understood as the principle that individuals should have the possibility to organize their lives as they wish, to choose their own ends, and to realize them as they think best, is the greatest contribution of liberalism to modern society (p. 20)

The biases of liberal democratic governments are written into its 17th- and 18th-century founding documents. Locke named men and property explicitly as privileged values in his *Second Treatise of Civil Government*. In the Enumeration Clause of the original U.S. Constitution, "other persons" (African slaves) were to be counted as 3/5 citizens in determining how many representatives a state would be allotted. (Native Americans were not counted at all.) Although some government values have changed since those documents were written, women's and African Americans' enfranchisement was guaranteed only during the 20th century, and U.S. citizens elected their first African American president and the first woman was appointed as Speaker of the House of Representatives during the 21st century. In 1886, the U.S. Supreme Court recognized corporations as people for the purposes of equal protection clauses of the 14th Amendment (*Santa Clara County v. Southern Pacific Railroad* 18 US 394), and in 2010, it granted them unlimited First Amendment rights in campaign financing (*Citizens United v. Federal Election Commission*,

130 S.CT 876). According to Frances Moore Lappé (2006), "The share of Americans who feel that the government is run by a few big interests looking out for themselves more than doubled since the 1960s to reach 76 percent" (p. 7). The inability or unwillingness of democratic government to be just toward all groups undermines the theoretical rational for liberal democracy. Why join the contract, if your rights are systematically subordinated (Cohen, 2010)?

At an individual level, reading with sociological imagination enables us to investigate the main effects and subtleties of current liberal democratic practices, which provide rhetorical support for freedom and equality, but provide little of their reality. Reading citizens can engage the public pedagogies of institutions and groups that attempt to position us all according to proscribed definitions of normality in private matters and push us toward consensus definitions of freedom and equality in public ones. By reading with sociological imagination, individuals have additional ways to choose to accept those combinations of positions of power and subordination or to name them as their main dangers. Sociological imagination helps us to appreciate the complex relationships between our personal and the social. As first steps toward democracy, we can name the dangers of the common good to our liberal rights to live differently, and we can choose the bias of governments toward certain groups as a main danger to our democratic rights to participate and be treated equally. In these ways, readers with sociological imagination don't seek to replace liberal democracy; rather, they look for ways to realize the promises of liberal democracy in more and more areas of their political and social lives.

I am not claiming that reading with sociological imagination will forge a new universal, fixed democratic identity that will finally cut through the ideological barriers that keep groups apart in order to form a new consensus on a correct normal life. Rather, I'm suggesting that reading with sociological imagination affirms pluralism, names conflicting interests of groups and institutions, identifies biased regularities in governments' actions, and commits to dissensus. By inviting more and more citizens to articulate their differences, politics of dissensus takes seriously the freedoms promised in liberal pluralism, locating those differences in relation to each other; identifying how consensus definitions privilege some groups and marginalize others; and legitimizing the conflicts among different groups that struggle to be recognized culturally, socially, and economically in order to be treated as equal, normal, and capable (Fraser, 2010). Reading with sociological imagination is a tool within the politics of dissensus because it expects difference, partisanship, conflict, and complexities and cautions us about the dangers in all ideas, values, and practices we bring to negotiations.

Rather than splitting a populace into groups with fixed, hard-boundary identities leading to the war of all against all, as feared in liberal theory, politics of dissensus relies on the fact that all of us are members of many groups with multiple and intersecting identities and discourses, and therefore we can recognize that our opponents in one political, social, cultural or economic conflict could become our allies in another. Thus a conflict of recognition and redistribution is not personal or permanent; it's just democratic practice. No groups or individuals can be taken for granted to toe the party line. Reading with sociological imagination within a politics of dissensus facilitates our liberal freedoms and democratic equality. Mouffe (2009), again:

> It is therefore crucial to realize that, with modern democracy, we are dealing with a new form of political society whose specificity comes from the articulation between two different traditions. On the one side we have the liberal tradition constituted by rule of law, the defense of human rights and the respect of individual liberty; on the other the democratic tradition, whose main ideas are those of equality, identity between governing and governed and popular sovereignty. There is no necessary relation between those two distinct traditions but only a contingent historical articulation. (p. 3)

Reading with sociological imagination encourages active and skillful participation in efforts to realize the promises of that contingent historical articulation. By helping citizens to recognize the complexities of the personal and its multiple connections to the social distribution of recognition and resources, reading with sociological imagination promotes a definition of citizenship as a daily commitment to choose which of our affinities to reaffirm and which of them to challenge because they have become too dangerous to our abilities to live and work with our different visions of normal life (Honig, 2009). Because new groups are always forming and old ones are finding new spaces in which to express their differences, articulations of democracy are continuously developing and expanding. If we take liberal pluralism and equality seriously, as many Americans say that they do, then we can take nothing for granted. We are thrust into the necessary and ongoing conflicts of dissensus through which we can make democracy daily in our lives. This brings new meaning to the phrase *government by the people.*

Yet the spatial scope of our understanding of the social and the realities of conflicts are shifting within the ongoing processes of globalization. As Ferdinand Tonnies (1887/2001) wrote about in the 19th century, the tensions between local negotiations of traditional practices and the national focus of modern relationships continue, but now they take place within and are influenced by transnational economic, social, and even political negotiations (Harvey, 1990). As the negotiations between the father and son in the Swat Valley and the pope and Catholic women around the world attest, traditional structures are still active and powerful. Modern structures continue to pit science against faith, progress against sustainability, and urban against rural. More and more, however, these unequal but reciprocal negotiations between the traditional and the modern take place within complex global contexts. Whether globalization is defined from the bottom up through postcolonial struggles for recognition and redistribution or from the top-down practices of trans- (not multi-) national corporate supply chains and nongovernmental agencies of finance, emerging globalizing structures enable and disable different visions of normality, of recognition, and of redistribution. Because the local (traditional) and the national (modern) still have influence on the global, Eric Swyngedouw (1997) names our current times as *glocalization*. Echoing Tonnies, Lemert (2004) labels this disruption of traditional and modern spatial, cultural, political, and economic structures to be a crisis:

> Strictly speaking, a crisis is any moment in the course of events when structured things of various kinds come to a turning point. All structures—prevailing weather patterns, planetary orbits, states or markets, championship teams, marriages or their equivalent, dollhouses, and so on—come to their turning points, which are, in effect, occasions when the structures must either change or get out of the way for better or worse. Weathers and planets reshuffle themselves, states and markets carry on until voted or sold out, champions grow old, dollhouses and marriages are left behind. (p. 212)

IMAGINING PEDAGOGY

The glocal (global/local) resonates within my classroom. American public schools are spaces where the local/traditional, national/modern, and global /postmodern collide. Put too simply, traditional teacher/student relationships of authority reside within and push against the bureaucratic hierarchies of schools in order to engage to varying degrees with new globally competitive curricula. Although wannabe teachers and teachers studying to be reading specialists are often familiar with the glocality of schools (yes, I am having fun with this new term), few teachers have explicit language for discussing how that context helps them remake democracy in and out of schools. By discussing, and even debating, the glocal, I hope to provide spaces in which to make our language more specific, more explicit, and more supportive of our efforts to use the openness of our identities as teachers. In order to ensure their engagement, we take up the ongoing transition of federal educational policy from No Child Left Behind to Race to the Top/Blueprint for Reform. In particular, we've focused on the new official goal for public schools—all students will graduate from high school either college or career ready. To make the reflective nature of our discussions visible, I ask them to hold up connection (agree) or conflict (disagree) index cards when appropriate as we talk through the issues of transition. It's awkward at first, but my students report that it encourages them to listen more carefully and to reflect on their values.

Invariably, we begin with connection cards flashing because a class member declares that teachers ultimately control curriculum because they "bring it to their students." Regardless of official policies, they agree, teachers mediate the topics and experiences for their students while in class. Solidarity slips and conflict cards emerge when some begin to argue that students mediate classroom curriculum as well. Typically, at least in my classes, all teachers concur about student involvement by raising their connections cards after such statements. After such soft conflicts appear and are resolved, someone will note aloud that conflict is unwelcome in their workplace or other classes. As they tell it, school officials or course instructors try to avoid conflict, positioning teachers as consumers of expert opinion or legitimate authority. All acknowledge that such efforts do not end conflict, but rather conceal it behind the assumption of consensus among the silent. Over time, some admit that they and most others accept these subordinate positions, and then, demonstrate perfectly how power circulates in schools by stating, "I close my doors and do my own thing," or the undergraduate equivalent, "I cram for the test and forget everything when the course is over." Lots of connection cards wave, but democracy in schools and classrooms suffers.

Yet on substantive matters, even this facade of a unified teacher identity begins to crumble. For example, some teachers argue for absolute local control for goals and curriculum because their school districts have high graduation rates, and their students find work locally, join the military, or enroll in further schooling. "This is what our parents want—for their kids to stay or come home." Other teachers cite high unemployment rates in their communities and the loss of "good jobs" locally as their rationale for advocating state or national goals, standards, and curricula. "Young people will have to leave the Happy Valley some day, and must have competitive skills when they go." After discussions, all seem to agree that their opponents make good points, providing clear and legitimate rationales in order to support their positions. At such moments if no else jumps in, I intervene in order to make three points explicitly:

1. Conflicts are always present.
2. Connections are always present.
3. This is democratic practice.

The acknowledgment of legitimate, but not easily reconcilable, differences pushes at the binary that I established at the outset of the class discussion—either conflict or connection. In this example, the complex tensions between learning to stay and learning to leave require that class members hold up both cards simultaneously. They seem to feel, not just think about, that tension toward the end of these discussions. Although they conflicted with other classmates concerning whose position is "realistic," "right," or "the future," they connected with all members that these positions are legitimate ways for teachers to think about their work and their responsibilities. They respect each other's positions because they are well argued and plausible. Their actions and tensions are the crux of dissensus. And I note that they have been naming differences, locating them, and searching for ways to live and work with those differences.

Class members have already demonstrated some of those ways during our discussion. While they noted differences and affinities with others during class discussion, they articulated their differences and affinities with citizens and institutions beyond our classroom and their schools as well. "That's what our parents want" is clearly an overstatement, essentializing a complex community into a consensus position, but it does imply some common ground between themselves and some local citizens and groups. Within their claim of solidarity with "outsiders," they demonstrate that they believe their personal issues around curricular control are really social problems, which cut across different identities in their community—teacher, parent, businessperson, conservative, activist, and too many more to list—who've come to the same conclusions from different vantage points. Of course, their opponents within the class discussion, who declared that "they'll have to leave" and other positions in between these two extremes find conflicts and connections across the glocal as well. Our capacities to identify with others and to explore our connections with them as potential main dangers provide opportunities for coalitions to form, strengthening and broadening the legitimacy of their shared readings of the situation and leading to greater participation in the decisions to follow. There are always possible connections, if we remain open to them.

Individuals' multiple, shifting identities and reflexivity reduce the likelihood that these single-issue coalitions will become fixed or permanent, subordinating opponents and imposing a new consensus. For example, the connections over school curriculum do not guarantee connections on other school or social, economic, cultural, and political issues. Members of a coalition to adopt the National Governors' Association's Common Core Standards of Race to the Top/Blueprint for Reform could splinter over the accompanying proposed standardized testing, and these new groups might split further, over the property tax increases required to implement the curriculum and tests in local schools. Through these subsequent discussions, teachers prove to themselves that new conflicts, connections, and coalitions will follow, act, and break part. And this process will proceed toward democracy as long as they continue to read with sociological imagination in and out of schools. Similar to our lives and educations, democracy is never complete—it's always in the making.

Although the topic of policy transition is generative—take up the emerging federal definition of a teaching career through its advocacy of Teach for America and charter schools if you want to see fur fly—the imaginative pedagogy comes through the discussion itself and explicit efforts to develop a language for talking about the roles for reading with sociological imagination in the continuous making of democracy. When buttressed by reason and emotion through reading the public pedagogies of social texts, conflicts become the "dynamics of pluralist democracy" (Mouffe, 1995), leading simultaneously to naming difference from some and locating similarities with others in order to form coalitions around clearly articulated alternatives. The openness of our identities and the reflexivity of readers guard against the tyranny of a permanent majority and new false consensus about the normal way to live, increasing the possibilities that we can learn to live and work with our differences in more and more parts of our lives.

OUT OF THE HAPPY VALLEY

We cannot be consumers of democracy, as the texts of my drive home from Grinnell tried to teach me. Expert opinion has its place; nostalgia is fun at times (dance on, Beaver faithful); and even spectacle can entertain us for a while. We can listen and learn, but we cannot accept the positions offered by these texts that tell us to turn away from civic life because it's boring, we're not smart enough to understand, and we should seek only comfort and security for ourselves. We must be producers of democracy by reading with sociological imagination, thinking daily about the main dangers in our lives, and forming coalitions in order to become democratic agents, imagining not what is, but what might be. The crisis in democracy throughout our lives is not about conflicts—pluralism means that conflict is permanent. Our democratic crisis comes because we have not been able to harness conflict's dynamic capacity. We have traditional, modern, and postmodern tools at our disposal in order to act locally, nationally and globally—all wrapped together in our glocal lives.

In previous chapters, I've shared the work of some individuals and groups reading toward democracy. For example, the groups debating the future of the Spring Creek Canyon held small group meetings in churches, town halls, and near the site; they marshaled evidence to characterize the validity of their claims; and they opened Facebook pages to display their position pictographically and to capture the comments of "friends." The National Geographic Society's campaign against rectangular coordinate maps tied the science and art of cartography to the political conflicts of representation, reaching across social science experts, government agencies, and educational institutions in order to quell the distortions of space, place, and environment. Playwright Norman Yeung and the new Situationists (e.g., Adbusters, Guerilla Girls, etc.) use the arts to interrogate social texts, to highlight conflicts, and to spark conversations among various audiences. All pursue self-interest (Canyon use, enhanced geographic awareness, and design) and all seek expanded notions of normal life (debate, inclusion, conflict, and participation). These individuals and groups act on their senses of what might be.

Acts of reading toward democracy are all around us. In Cleveland, the six neighborhoods that constitute the Greater University Circle are filled with hollow factories, empty houses, and vacant storefronts. Area unemployment is over 25%, home foreclosures have sucked much of the wealth from the neighborhoods, and 30% of the residents live below the poverty line. Wary of lectures on lack of moral character, the calls for tax breaks for corporations willing to move into enterprise zones, and job-training centers that prepare the unemployed for work in other regions, members of the Cleveland Foundation sought programs that would simultaneously enhance the prospects of the community, its established institutions, and its 43,000 inhabitants. Working with large anchor institutions (Case Western Reserve University, University Hospital, the Cleveland Clinic, and others), local churches, and neighborhood associations, they established the Evergreen Cooperatives based on the notion that community businesses could keep some of the anchor institutions' $3 billion goods and services budget local.

To date, the coalition has established four cooperative businesses (Evergreen, Ohio Solar, City Green, and Neighborhood Voice) to provide laundry, solar panels and weatherproofing, and greenhouse lettuce and herbs for the anchor institutions, and local news and culture for the community. Employees are recruited from the neighborhoods; earn a living wage and no-cost health benefits; and after six months, become vested as stock-earning owners of the companies. Once vested, employees enjoy the right to participate in all company decision making. Currently the industries are small (25 employees each), but their plans are large. Leaders and partners have visited the Mondragon Cooperative Corporation in the Basque region of Spain, which is the world's largest organization of cooperatives with over 100 industries with 120,000 employee/owners and more than $21 billion in sales. Fifty years ago the Basque was impoverished—with a sparse, unskilled labor force and little industry or infrastructure. Today the cooperatives have stabilized the region, provided authentic rationales for schooling and training, increased democratic principles among the population, and achieved sustainability through real market forces. In Cleveland, the Evergreen Cooperatives' market plan is to scale up the win-win relationships between the community businesses and the anchor institutions until the revenue reaches a tipping point when enough wealth and stability has been created in the neighborhoods that new unaffiliated businesses (and jobs) will be attracted to the community. That point is imagined to be 10 cooperative businesses with 5,000 local employee/owners, leading to more employment and stability.

The Evergreen Cooperatives or Cleveland Model is a darling of a wide spectrum of news media from *The Economist* to *The Nation* (with NBC and NPR in between)—all of which represent this project as a possible solution for urban blight. And it could well be, but it rests on the abilities of several groups to find and maintain continuous connections across their differences. First, the anchor institutions must choose, perform, and maintain this role of responsible community members, changing their current corporate practices of purchasing these goods and services from national, even international, subcontractors at the lowest possible prices and transporting them through the neighborhoods. Second, the community must believe the sincerity of this proposed institutional change, overcoming 50 years of mistrust stemming from reading other repeated, failed corporate and government solutions to urban problems in general and their neighborhoods' decline in particular. Third, workers must leave the existing neighborhood economies and loyalties currently in place in order to commit to the Evergreen ways, believing that the promise of democratic employment will materialize and continue into the future. Incentives for all groups seem to be in place. The anchor institutions receive the goods and services, the environmental features of reducing their carbon footprint (and corresponding tax breaks), and the prospects of stable neighborhoods in the Greater University Circle. Members of the community have new opportunities for employment (500 applications for each job so far) that promises to treat them with the respect of participation in the decision making about their work, company direction, and the future of their neighborhood. Beyond those employees, community groups and members have new hope—that's a remarkable incentive.

Deserted barns and fallow fields are the rural equivalent of idle factories and vacant city houses. Many of the families who once worked those farms have moved on to other places in order to make their living. In and around the Happy Valley, at least, rural ways of living seem under siege from corporate farms and transnational food supply chains. The tensions manifest themselves in various ways. For example, some of the people whom I interviewed for a study on rural literacies and the fight against corporate hog farms in Pennsylvania remain on their land. At least one, however, locked his hogs in the barn and vanished (Shannon, 2004). As more and more families leave farms, the towns that supported them and were supported by them slowly shrink. The members of the Pennsylvania Association for Sustainable Agriculture (PASA) work to develop coalitions among people who read those empty barns, abandoned fields, and waning towns as the main danger of rural lives.

To be sustainable, farmers need consistent markets for their yields without encouragement for overdevelopment and excessive debt. PASA began in 1991 with plans for local networks of farmers' markets, Buy Fresh Buy Local programs, and crop share projects across the valleys of the Susquehanna in order to connect farmers and consumers as directly as possible. The early work required the personal touch of PASA members visiting small local farms in order to invite participation and attending meetings of town councils, restaurant owners, and community groups to organize the markets. Behind their advocacy of "safe, sane, sustainable, and fair food systems," they offered courses on environmentally friendly farming, sponsored an annual Farming for the Future conference, and led farm tours and field days for intensive learning of new techniques. At present, the valleys' network includes 59 participating farmers, 21 farmers markets, 19 restaurants, and 8 retailers, and PASA has branches in seven regions across the state. Its annual conference attracts 2,000 people from across the United States.

Although the romantic notion of the yeoman farmer has a long history in the United States, the PASA initiative rubs directly against three overlapping popular discourses. The first area of conflict is scale—small independent farms cannot produce sufficiently to feed all Americans. This was the argument for the introduction of corporate hog farms in Pennsylvania a decade ago, and its advocates have met the PASA project with the frame "boutique farming." A second discourse of conflict is freedom of choice—local farms can't supply asparagus in November. Farm share means a fall of squash recipes. The third conflict is over price—across the valleys we're told to "save money, live better." Buying fresh and local costs more, and many people in rural, suburban, and urban areas have very hard choices to make about how to spend their money. PASA meets these conflicts head on, trying to find connections among the people who use these discourses by asking, "How do you want to live?" in as many venues as they meet people.

To demonstrate some possibilities of a Buy Fresh, Buy Local project, PASA opened a small restaurant in an empty storefront beneath its administrative office in Millheim, Pennsylvania. This effort required a different set of negotiations, bringing together bankers, business owners—particularly established restaurant and bar owners—and townspeople to shape the business plan. The negotiated decision was to open and serve local fare on only Friday and Saturday nights and Sunday afternoons, with local artists' work on the walls and local musicians entertaining from 7:00 to 9:00 at night and 1:00 to 3:00 on Sundays. Beyond PASA's economic, social, and environmental agendas, the restaurant became a cultural space in which local arts and rural agendas could mix. (Kathleen and I spent part of our 20th wedding anniversary at the restaurant, listening to the Nightcrawlers.) During the past 5 years, the restaurant has become independent from PASA, tripled in size, and engaged in community politics and cultural life.

Small towns are diverse places. Looking out the wide windows of the expanded restaurant, you can see this fact represented on the street: a take-out pizza shop; an old bank (now a branch); Brownies, a brick-front tavern with slit windows crowded with neon beer signs; a storefront post office; and the Millheim Hotel (built in 1794). Often, you can witness a tractor-trailer drive through town with an Amish family in their enclosed buggy following behind. On the street, before the restaurant opens and after it closes, the locally networked farmers and customers meet community members who do not farm and moved to the area to keep expenses low, people whose families have lived in the region for generations, and the ultimate "other" in rural life—the Amish. While all seek to enjoy the benefits of pluralist democracy and live their lives as they see fit, if the town is to survive, they must also find ways to learn to live together with their differences. At this point, the success of the restaurant has attracted new businesses to fill some of the empty stores along the town's main street and new cultural events have moved from the restaurant to the town's public spaces—the shores of Elk Creek, the park, and school grounds.

The possibilities of drilling for natural gas in the Marcellus Shale are reshuffling the coalitions across the valleys and complicating Millheim's daily negotiations of its rural plurality. PASA's efforts to connect the concept of foodshed with the Chesapeake Bay Watershed in locals' minds confront national and international demand for energy and the possibilities of some landowners' signing lucrative contracts with drilling companies. Pennsylvanians have a long history of harvesting the state's natural resources in order to supply the region, nation, and world with lumber, coal, oil, and now natural gas. New debates spin discourses around land management and zoning, ownership, methods of extraction, water use and pollution, government responsibility, infrastructure, and taxation. All citizens seem well aware of the $1 trillion estimated site value of the gas and the jump in local revenues gained from the expenses surrounding the well construction and drilling. For those who have been wondering about the viability of rural lives for decades, drilling for natural gas appears to be a new way to sustain rural life and bring those ideas and interest to the conversations.

PieLab is a cautionary tale, and perhaps, a success story. Currently, it's a restaurant in Greensboro, Alabama, that provides job training, a "neutral space" for conversation among townspeople, and . . . well, pie. It began in Belfast, Maine, when a small group of young socially conscious graphic designers calling themselves Project M (www.projectmlab.com) scribbled its formula on the back of a cocktail napkin:

PieLab = a neutral place + a slice of pie.
A neutral space + a slice of pie = conversation
Conversation = ideas + design
Ideas + design = positive change.

Their work for Hale County, Alabama, began with a highly successful graphic design project that raised $40,000 for water meters needed to bring running water to area homes. At the invitation of a local community organization, five members of Project M moved to Greensboro and opened PieLab as a temporary shop in which locals of all varieties could meet for pie and conversation (begin the formula). From these chance meetings new projects would emerge. The first lab was in the kitchen of a local residence—on the first day, they made $400 at 2 bucks a slice. Within 6 months, PieLab was a storefront pie restaurant with imitators in many cities across the country and BikeLab in its old space. Design + media savvy = growth.

Conflict between Project M and some locals arose almost immediately around the original Buy a Meter campaign. To draw attention to the cause and raise donations, Project M represented the Hale County population as impoverished, poorly educated, and lacking in compassion ("Water is not a right in Hale County"). Some community members resented that characterization. Once PieLab opened and began to draw more young designers to town, intergenerational conflicts developed over dress, manners, and acceptable behaviors. As relations between PieLab workers and some community members became more contentious and more public, Project M excused itself from the shop, leaving several locals in charge of the workspace and eliciting changes to its current form. In one sense, PieLab's formula didn't work as planned, because the young designers didn't keep up their end of the conversation—apparently unable or unwilling to find lasting connections with locals to help design new projects. Without the conversations, ideas, design, and change could not follow. Looked at in another way, however, Project M didn't write itself as a variable in the original PieLab formula, and from that vantage point, the ensuing conflict was a catalyst that enabled the locals to make the formula for designing change their own.

Despite the obvious differences among Evergreen, PASA, and PieLab projects, the participants are reading the signs of abandonment—closed factories, empty barns, and vacant town square—with sociological imagination. They are questioning the preferred interpretations of abandoned buildings as the necessary consequences of economic, social, cultural, and political innovations or unfortunate indicators of the inabilities of some individuals (and cultures) to change with the times. They are rejecting the positions those idle spaces and those apologists offer them in order to explore what other meanings are possible when readers start with the assumption that the abandonment they see is indicative of social problems, and not personal issues to be overcome by individuals' bootstrap behaviors. They are noting that the benefits and consequences of abandonment are not being distributed equally among groups in their communities. Whether or not the participants are personally comfortable despite the conditions of abandonment, they are pushing past reading only for social competence and are locating the particular discourses that excuse and facilitate the production of abandonment in its many physical, human, and discursive forms. And they are recognizing the many groups—some of which they are members of—who are performing these enabling discourses in their communities.

Rather than seeing only what is, they are imagining what might be— an urban collaboration between responsible institutions and responsive neighborhoods; a food/watershed that makes rural life viable for farmers and consumers; and a town driven by conversation, ideas, and change. None of these projects are springing fully formed from the heads of any individual or group. Each is requiring continued negotiation of definitions, strategies, and actions among participants and other interested parties, leading to the prospects of temporary coalitions among groups over particular articulations. Each decision to be made is being weighed according to the different material and discursive interests of the members of coalitions involved. In these ways, they are learning how to live and work with those differences. When decision making ignores those interests, things fall apart and new efforts must be made to seek and keep difference. Adding to the tentativeness of these projects are the historical structures and discourses that are mediating against participants' attempts to disrupt the binaries of neighborhoods and institutions, traditions and change, and insiders and outsiders to form coalitions. There are no guarantees of success, or even likelihood that the participants could agree on what success looks and feels like. Shifting circumstances are ensuring that the projects will never be finally made, but will always be in the making.

I find these examples to be inspiring; inviting; and, I'll admit, a little bit daunting. I appreciate the content of their projects—participants seem eager to promote and protect different ways of living normally and expanded participation in the decisions that affect their lives, imagining how diverse human needs for recognition and more equitable distribution of benefits and consequences could be met within communities. From my distant reading, what keeps these participants active without guarantees are their daily ethico-political choices about the main dangers in their lives. As they read the social things around them, they fear the consequences of civic apathy sufficiently to look for connections with others on most days in order to produce more democracy in their lives and the lives of others.

The participants are good reading teachers as well. They demonstrate that reading with sociological imagination must be understood in the progressive tense. It's not a step toward democracy in the sense of a sequence, because each next step, each move, requires new readings of the texts and circumstances we find there. Reading is a continuous element of agency that cannot be separated from imagining what might be. They show that differences in the readings of the same text are what make the imagination possible. They seek participation in reading in order to invite difference—not just in the sense that "things could be different," but more for the generative capacity that happens when differences meet and stimulate thoughts of new possibilities of what we could "become." They illustrate how reason, desire, ethics, remembering, culture, and aesthetics combine while reading, bringing traditional, modern, and postmodern twists to meanings. By valuing these different ways of knowing, they offer multiple entry points to the text(s) they are producing daily.

My learning to read is a work in progress. Inquiry into my reading practices and the act of writing this book have identified roles for reading unimaginable when I started. I'm learning that all things are social, and therefore readable, as texts. Through practices of production, those social things are meant to teach me my position(s) in the world through the representations, frames, and discourses behind them. I feel wide awake to the tension between accepting things as they come down and investigating why they are the way they are. Each encounter with difference helps me question my rush to reach consensus and deepens my understanding of the possibilities of dissensus within pluralist democracy. Although new literacies and media increase the flows of these encounters, I've learned that they are social things affording traditional, modern, and postmodern practices and values simultaneously. I call my work in progress reading wide awake, and I recognize that others engage in this work, this reading as well.

The varieties of reading, text production, and pedagogy that we perform invite others to engage. Of course the word progress, as in work in progress, connotes that we have it all figured out and are advancing toward an identifiable goal. Although each has short-term objectives that are clearly indicated, none can specify all that a pluralistic democracy would or could be. Like our learning to read, democracy is always in the making. The creativity among increasingly diverse producers of texts and creative destruction in the communications industries will ensure that inquiries into our reading practices and democracy will remain continuous. Our current reading practices are all we have at our disposal to make our choices every day to determine which is the main danger. That's why we pin our hopes on reading toward democracy.

References

Atkinson, K. (2008). *When will there be good news?* New York: Little, Brown.

Bakhtin, M. (1990). *Art and answerability.* Austin: University of Texas.

Barthes, R. (1982). *A Barthes reader* (S. Sontag, Ed.). New York: Wang & Hill.

Baudrillard, J. (1988). *Selected writings* (M. Posner, Ed.). Palo Alto, CA: Stanford University.

Bauman, Z. (2000). *Liquid modernity.* New York: Polity.

Berliner, D. (2006). Our impoverished view of education reform. *Teachers College Record, 108*(6), 949–995.

Berliner, D. (2009). *Poverty and potential: Out of school factors and school success.* Boulder, CO: Education Public Interest Center. Available at http://nepc.colorado.edu/publication/poverty-and-potential

Boggs, S. (1947). Cartohypnosis. *Scientific Monthly, 64*(2), 469–476.

Bourdieu, P. (1977). *Outline of a theory of practice.* Cambridge: Cambridge University Press.

Bourdieu, P., & Wacquaint, L. (1994). *Invitation to reflexive sociology.* Chicago: University of Chicago Press.

Broache, A. (2007). Google updates map after Katrina airbrushing incident. Available at http://www.mail-archive.com/infowarrior@attrition.org/msg01799.html

Butler, J. (1993). *Bodies that matter.* New York: Routledge.

Children's Defense Fund. (2010). *State of America's children 2010.* Washington, DC: Author.

Cohen, C. (2010). *Democracy remixed.* New York: Oxford University Press.

Cott, J. (1983). *Pipers at the gates of dawn.* New York: McGraw-Hill.

Curtis, G. (2006). *The cave painters.* New York: Knopf.

Davies, B. (2000). *A body of writing: 1990–1999.* Lanham, MD: Alta Mira.

Davies, B., & Harre, R. (1990). Positioning: The discursive production of selves. *Journal for the Theory of Social Behavior, 20*(1), 43–63.

Debord, G. (1970). *The society of the spectacle.* New York: Black & White.

Fiske, J. (1989). *Reading the popular.* London: Unwin Hyman.

Foucault, M. (1970). *The order of things.* New York: Pantheon.

Foucault, M. (1973). *Birth of the clinic.* New York: Pantheon.

Foucault, M. (1983). On the genealogy of ethics. In H. Dreyful & P. Rabinow (Eds.), *Beyond structuralism and hermeneutics* (pp. 229–252). Chicago: University of Chicago.

Foucault, M. (1988). *Civilization and madness*. New York: Vintage. (Original work published 1961)

Foucault, M. (1991). *Discipline and punishment: The birth of prisons*. New York: Penguin. (Original work published 1975)

Fraser, N. (1996). *Justice interruptus*. New York: Routledge.

Fraser, N. (2000, May/June). Rethinking recognition. *New Left Review, 3*, 107–120. Available at http://www.newleftreview.org/?view=2248

Fraser, N. (2010). *Scales of justice*. New York: Columbia University Press.

Gilman, C. P. (1997). *The yellow wallpaper*. New York: Cover. (Original work published 1887)

Greer-Pitts, S. (2009). Obesity and air conditioning. Available at http://suesstew. blogspot.com/2009/06/social-issues-obesity-and-air.html

Groopman, J. (2007). *How doctors think*. Boston: Houghton Mifflin.

Hall, D., & Kennedy, S. (2006). *Primary progress, secondary challenge: A state by state look at student achievement patterns*. Washington, DC: Education Trust.

Hall, S. (1997). *Representation: Cultural representations and signifying practices*. New York: Open University Press.

Hall, S. (2003). *Listening to Stephen read*. New York: Open University Press.

Hamper, B. (1991). *Rivethead*. New York: Warner.

Harvey, D. (1990). *The conditions of postmodernity*. New York: Blackwell.

Harvey, D. (2010). Capitalism in crisis. Available at http://www.youtube.com/watch?v=qOP2V_np2c0

Hedges, C. (2009). *Empire of illusion: The end of literacy and the triumph of spectacle*. New York: Nation Books.

Heidegger, M. (1993). *Basic writings*. New York: HarperCollins. (Original work published 1954)

Herrnstein, R., & Murray, C. (1994). *The bell curve*. New York: Free Press.

Honig, B. (2009). *Emergency politics*. Princeton, NJ: Princeton University Press.

Iser, W. (1974). *The implied reader*. Baltimore, MD: Johns Hopkins University Press.

Jefferson, T. (1816, January 6). Letter to Colonel Charles Yancey. Available at http://memory.loc.gov/ammem/collections/jefferson_papers/

Johnson, B. (2010, January 11). Privacy no longer a social norm says Facebook founder. Available at http://www.guardian.co.uk/technology/2010/jan/11/facebook-privacy

Kaiser Family Foundation. (2010). *Generation M2: Media in the lives of 8 to 18 year olds*. Washington, DC: Author.

Keppel, F. (1965). *Aid to elementary and secondary education: Hearing before the General Subcommittee on Education of the Committee on Education and Labor, 89th Congress*. 1st Session. Washington, DC: U.S. Government Printing Office.

Kessler, F. (2000). A visual basic algorithm for the Winkel Tripel projection. *CaCIS, 21*(2), 28–35.

Kidd, D. C. (2009). Mortgages and sociological imagination. Available at http://dustinkidd.blogspot.com/2009/09/mortgages-and-sociological-imagination.html

Kneebone, E., & Garr, E. (2010). *The suburbanization of poverty*. Washington, DC: Brookings Institution.

Knobel, M., & Lankshear, C. (2007). *New literacies sampler.* New York: Peter Lang.

Kress, G. (2009). *Multimodality: A social semiotic approach to contemporary communications.* New York: Routledge.

Lacan, J. (1968). *The language of self: The function of language in psychoanalysis.* Baltimore, MD: Johns Hopkins University Press.

Lappé, F. M. (2006). *Democracy's edge.* San Francisco: Jossey-Bass.

Lee, J. (2006). *Tracking achievement gaps and assessing the impact of NCLB on the gap.* Cambridge, MA: Civil Rights Project of Harvard University.

Lemert, C. (2004). *Sociology after the crisis.* Boulder, CO: Paradigm.

Lemert, C. (2008). *Social things.* Lanham, MD: Rowman & Littlefield.

Leonard, A. (2008). The story of stuff. Available at http://www.storyofstuff.com/

Locke, J. (1986). *Second treaties of civil government.* Amherst, NY: Prometheus. (Original work published 1689)

Malcolm X. (1987). *The autobiography of Malcolm X.* New York: Ballantine. (Original work published 1967)

Marcuse, H. (1964). *One-dimensional man: Studies in the ideology of advanced industrial society.* Boston: Beacon.

Marx, K. (1969). *The 18th Brumaire of Louis Bonaparte.* New York: International. (Original work published 1852)

Masny, D., & Cole, D. (Eds.). (2009). *Multiple literacies theory.* New York: Sense.

McRobbie, A. (2002). A mixed bag of misfortunes: Bourdieu's weight of the world. *Theory, Culture and Society, 19*(3), 129–138.

Miller, B. (2007, March 30). Letter to Dr. Eric Schmidt. Available at http://democrats.science.house.gov/Media/File/AdminLetters/miller_google_katrina_maps-07mar30.pdf.

Mills, C. W. (1959). *The sociological imagination.* Chicago: University of Chicago Press.

Mitchell, W. J. T. (1995). *Picture this: Essays on visual and verbal representation.* Chicago: University of Chicago.

Monmonier, M. (1994). *Drawing lines: Tales of maps and cartoversy.* New York: Henry Holt.

Mouffe, C. (1995). Politics, democratic action, and solidarity. *Inquiry, 38*(1), 98–113.

Mouffe, C. (1996). Radical of liberal democracy. In D. Trend (Ed.), *Radical democracy* (pp. 19–27). New York: Routledge.

Mouffe, C. (2009). *Democratic paradox.* New York: Verso.

National Commission on Excellence in Education. (1983). *A nation at risk: The imperative for educational reform* [a report to the Nation and the Secretary of Education, United States Department of Education]. Washington, DC: Author. Available at http://www2.ed.gov/pubs/NatAtRisk/index.html

New London Group. (1996). A pedagogy of multiliteracies: Designing for the future. *Harvard Educational Review, 66*(1), 60–92.

Nisbett, R. (2009). *Intelligence and how to get it: Why school and culture count.* New York: Norton.

Numeroff, L. (1985). *If you give a mouse a cookie.* New York: Scholastic.

Packard, V. (2007). *The hidden persuaders.* New York: Ig. (Original work published 1957)

Peet, R. (2007). *Geographies of power*. New York: Zed.

Phillips, D., & Burbules, N. (2000). *Postpositivism and educational research*. Boulder, CO: Rowman & Littlefield.

Postman, N. (1982). *The disappearance of childhood*. New York: Delacorte.

Putnam, R. (Ed.). (2004). *Democracies in flux: The evolution of social capital in contemporary society*. New York: Oxford University Press.

Radosh, D. (2009, August 11). My guitar gently beeps. *New York Times*, p. MM26. Available at http://www.nytimes.com/2009/08/16/magazine/16beatles-t.html

Rich, F. (2009, December 19). Tiger Woods, person of the year. *New York Times*, p. WK7. Available at http://www.nytimes.com/2009/12/20/opinion/20rich.html

Robinson, A. (1990). Rectangular world maps—No! *Professional Geographer, 42*(1), 101–104.

Sandlin, J., Schultz, B., & Burdick, J. (Eds.). (2009). *The handbook of public pedagogy*. New York: Routledge.

Schumpeter, J. (1962). *Capitalism, socialism, and democracy*. New York: Harpers.

Shannon, P. (2004). The practices of democracy and Dewey's challenge. *Language Arts, 82*(1), 15–25.

Shelley, M. (2001). *Frankenstein; or, The modern Prometheus*. New York: Penguin. (Original work published 1818)

Simon, R. (1992). *Teaching against the grain*. Westport, CT: Bergin & Garvey.

Smith, D. (1998, May 30). Philosopher gamely in defense of his ideas. *New York Times*, Sec B, p. 7. Available at http://www.nytimes.com/1998/05/30/arts/philosopher-gamely-in-defense-of-his-ideas.html?src=pm

Swyngedouw, E. (1997). Neither global nor local: Glocalization and the politics of scale. In K. Cox (Ed.), *Spaces of globalization* (pp. 137–166). Minneapolis, MN: Guilford.

Tonnies, F. (2001). *Community and civil society*. New York: Columbia University. (Original work published 1887)

Voloshinov, V. (1973). *Marxism and the philosophy of language*. New York: Seminar.

Warren, S., & Brandeis, L. (1890). The right to privacy. *Harvard Law Review, 4*(5), 193–195. Available at http://groups.csail.mit.edu/mac/classes/6.805/articles/privacy/Privacy_brand_warr2.html

Weber, M. (1997). *Theory of social and economic organization* (A. Anderson & T. Parsons, Trans.). New York: Free Press. (Original work published 1947)

Williams, R. (1977). *Marxism and literature*. New York: Oxford University.

Index

About the Author

A former preschool and primary grade teacher, **Patrick Shannon** is a professor of education at Penn State University. He has worked in public schools and universities across the United States and Canada, and is currently working with Kathleen Collins and Kathleen Shannon to develop and study a sociocultural, multimodal alternative to RTI (Response to Intervention) for children and youth positioned as struggling to learn to read and write at school. The project is labeled Reading Camp (not Reading Clinic) and serves as part of the curriculum for reading specialist/special education certification candidates. He is in the process of rewriting his *Reading Poverty* (1998). Among his 16 books are *The Struggle to Continue* (1992), *text, lies, & videotape* (1995), and *Reading Against Democracy* (2007). He was elected to the Reading Hall of Fame in 2002.